This Book Belongs To

....

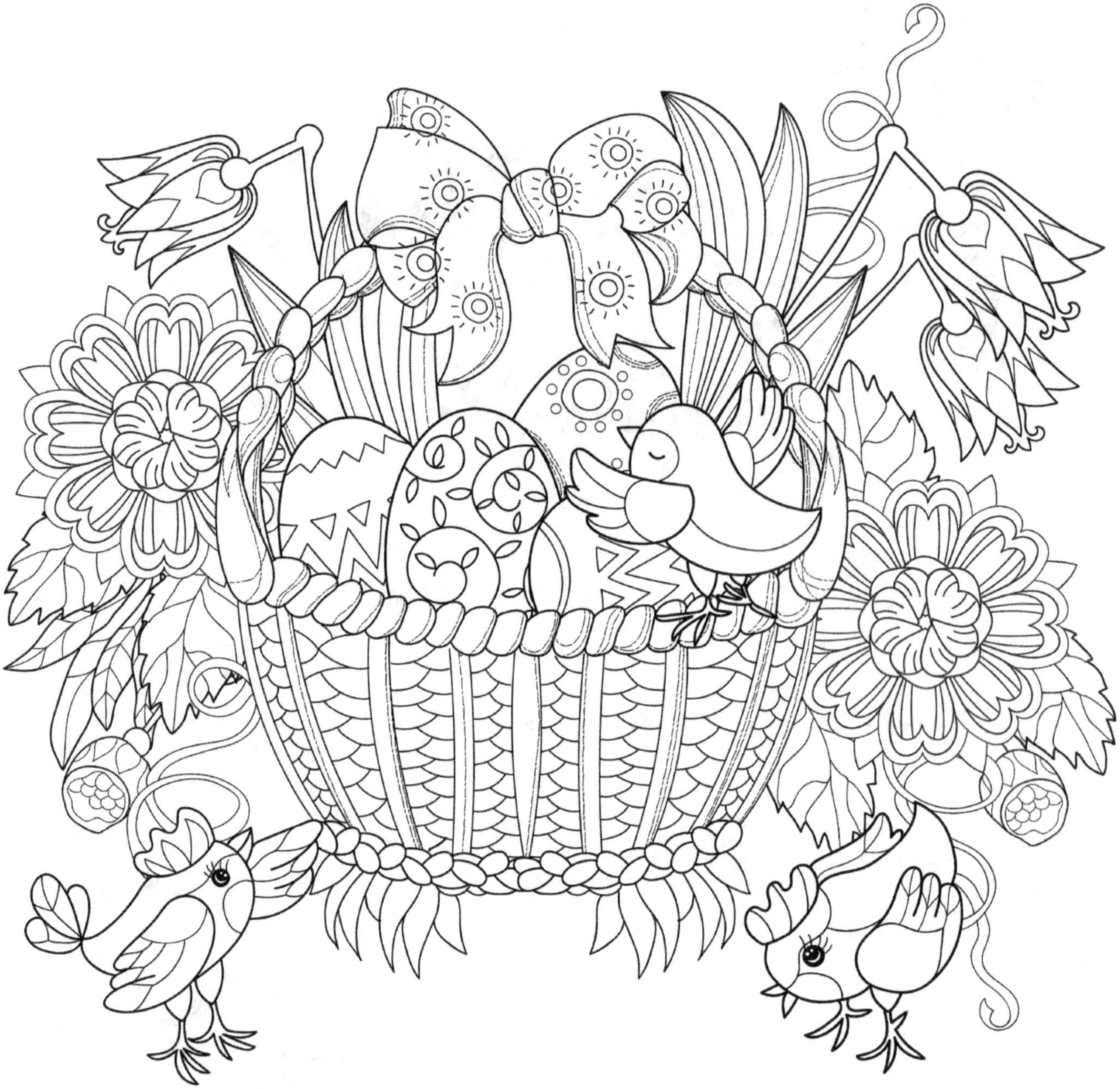

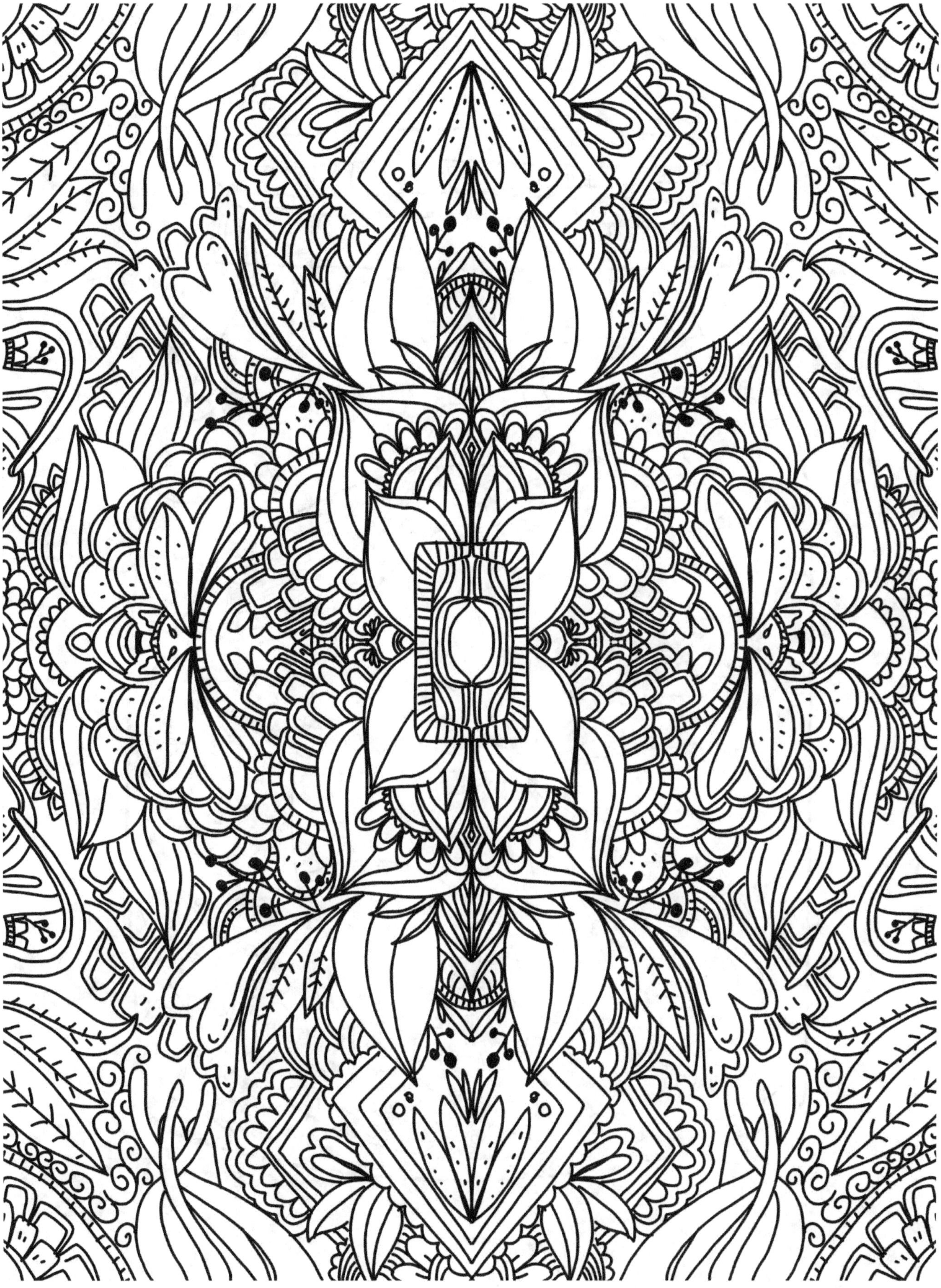

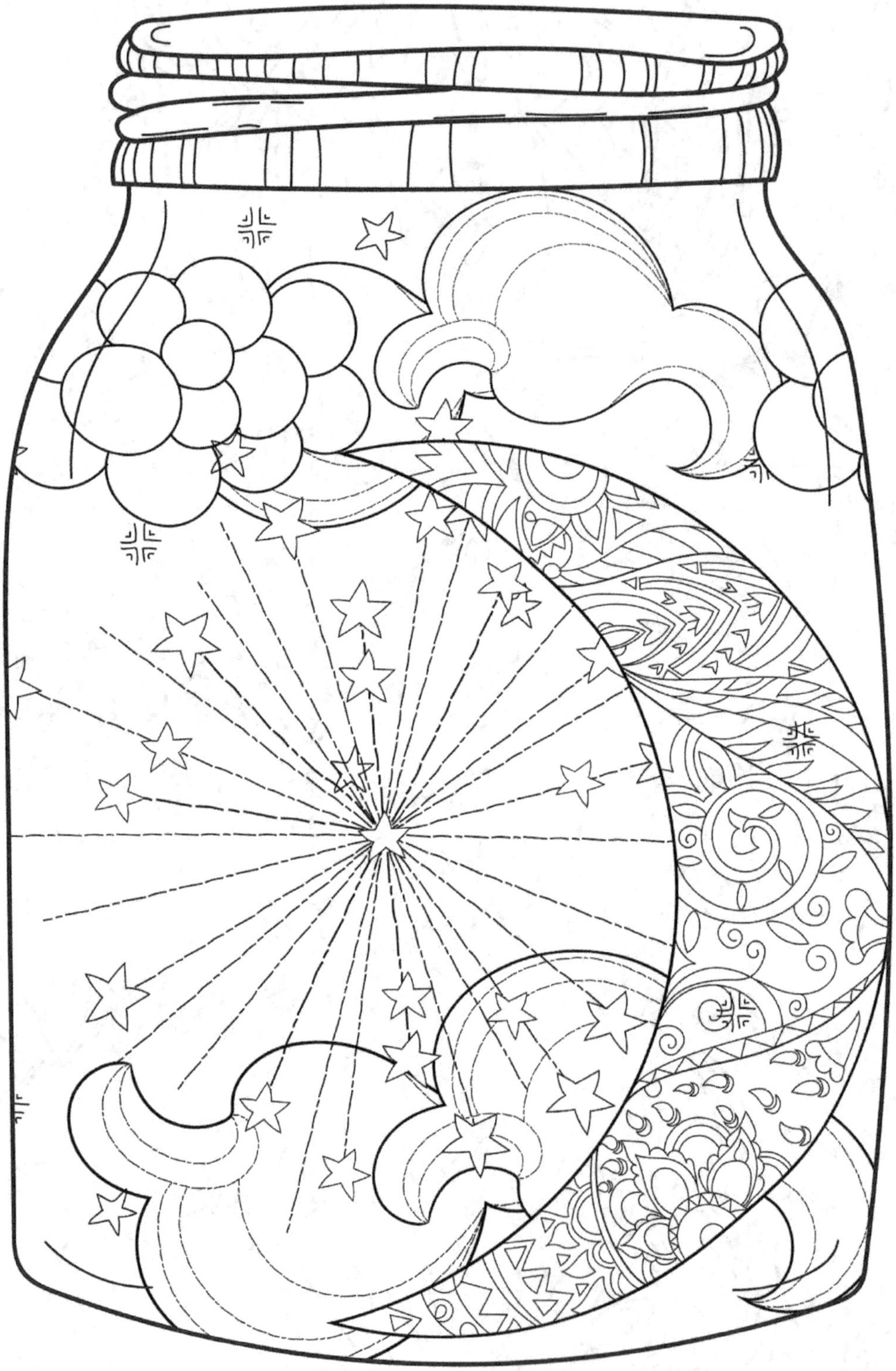

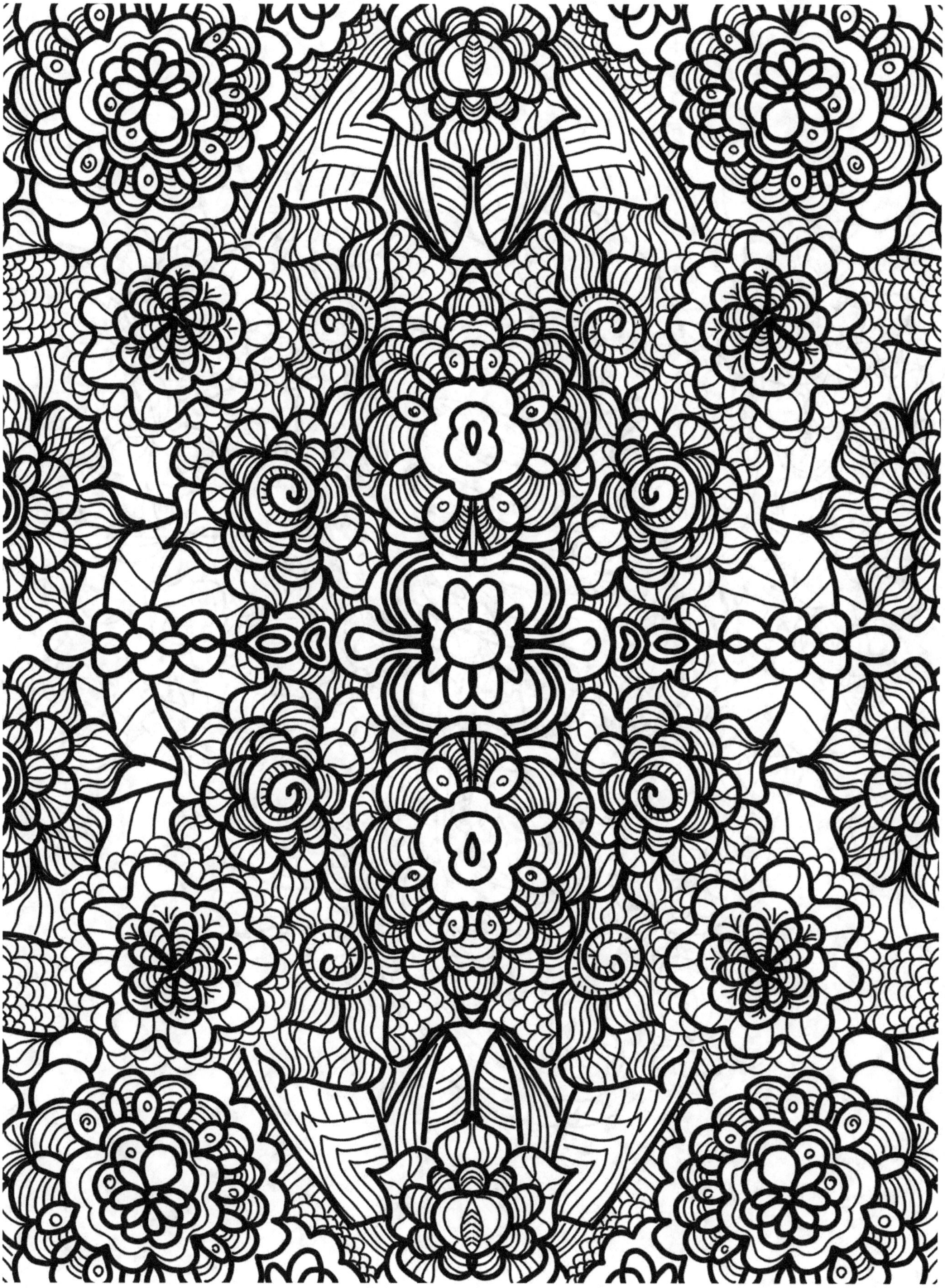

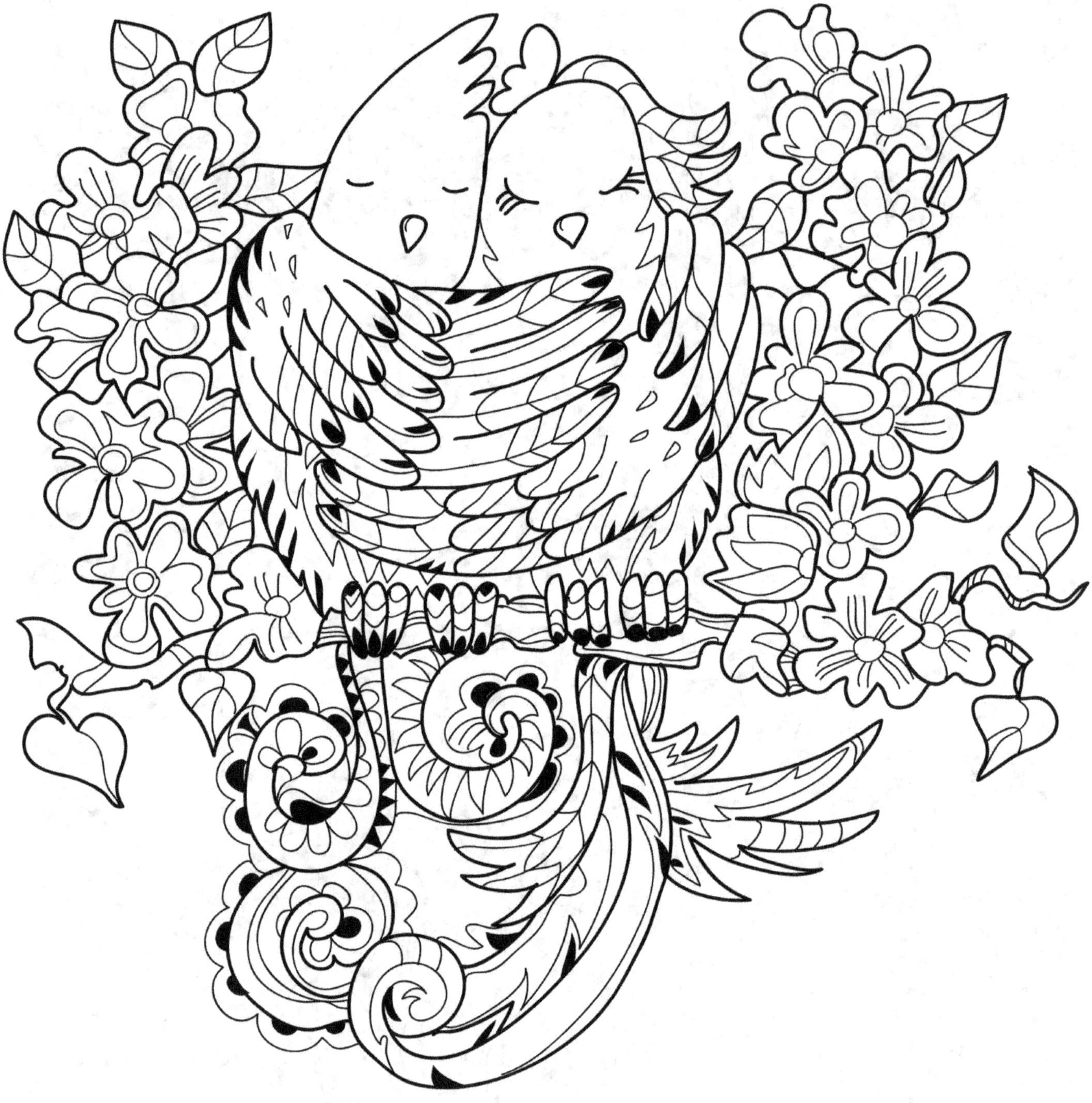

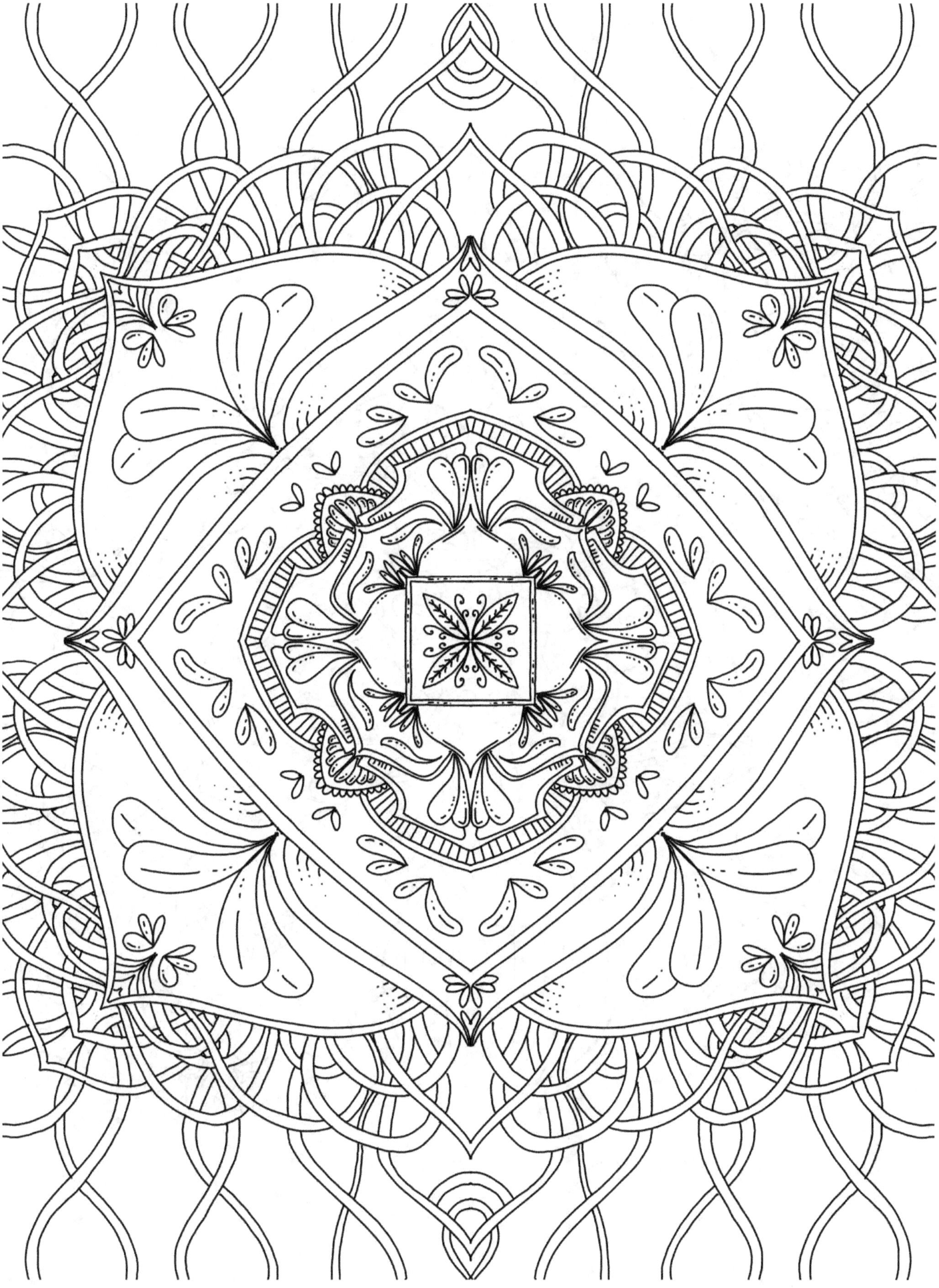

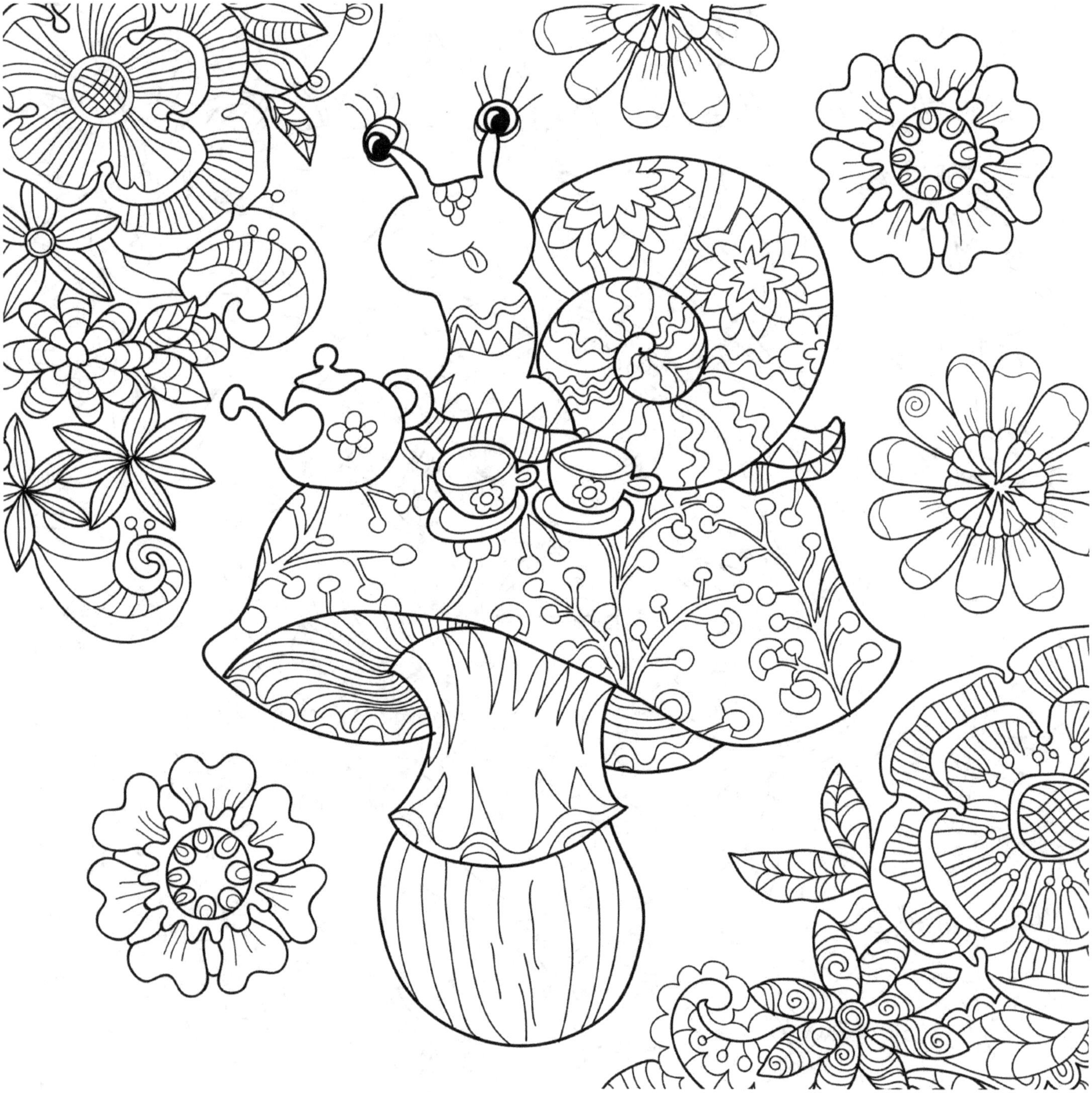

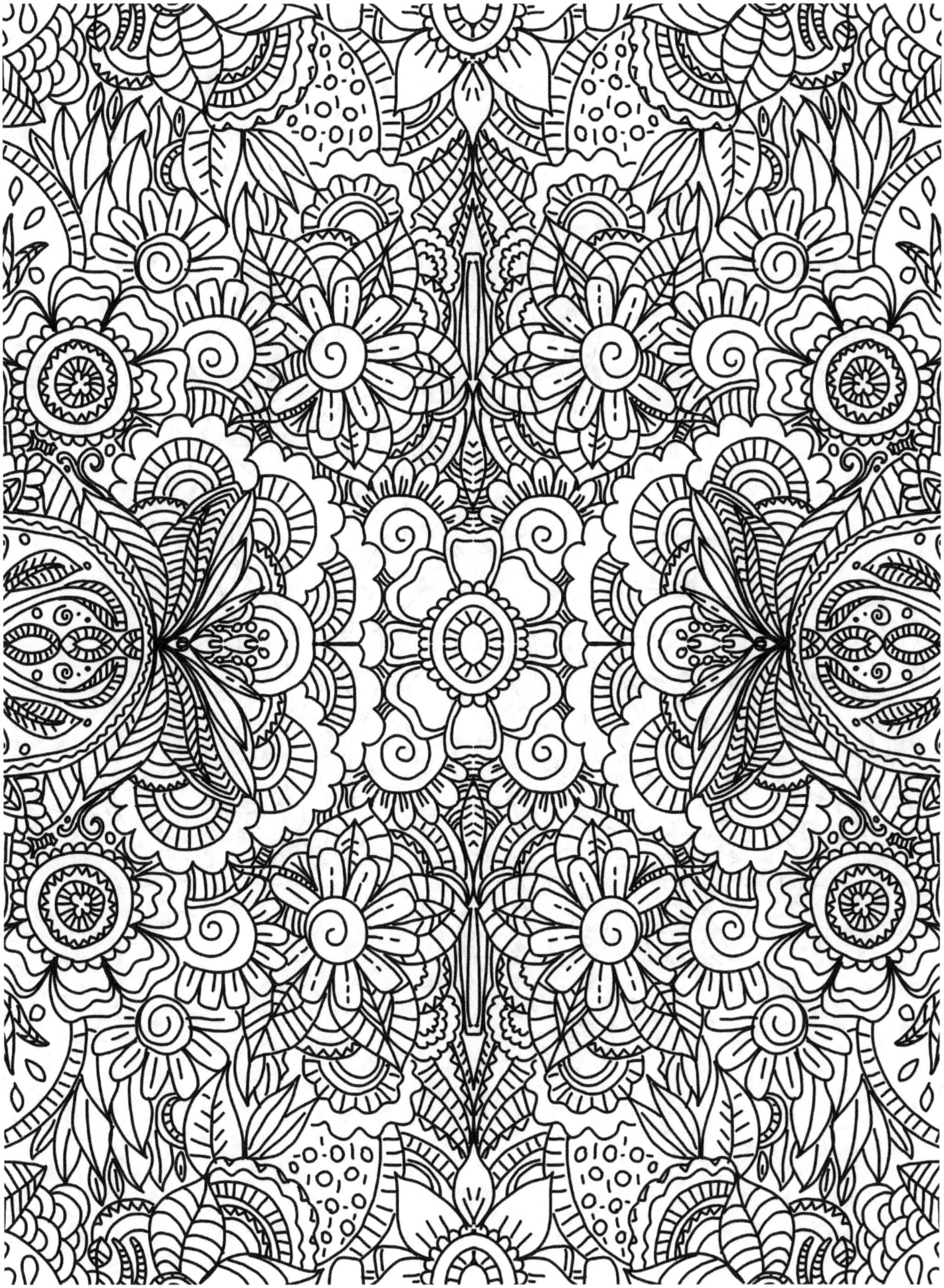

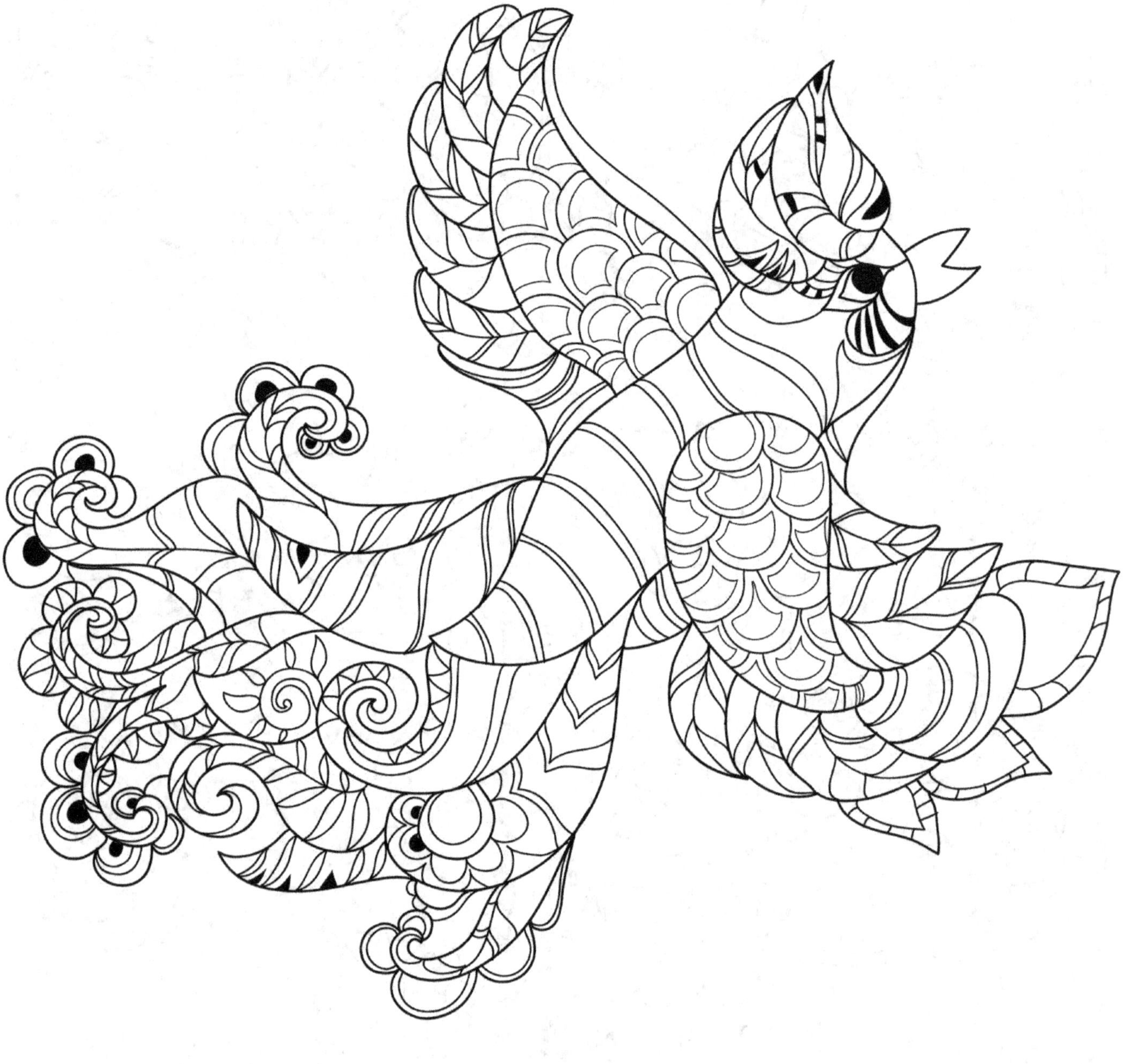

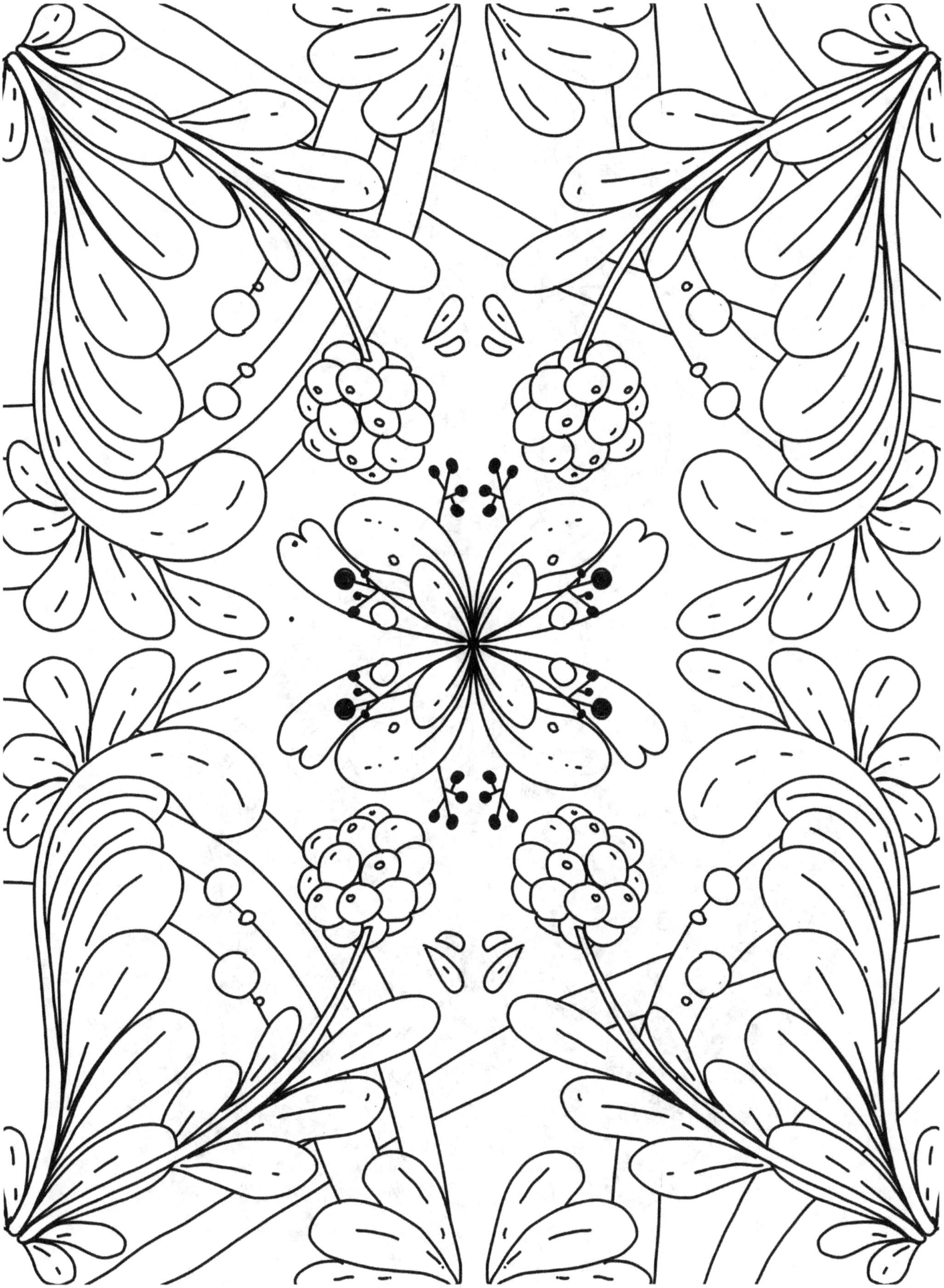

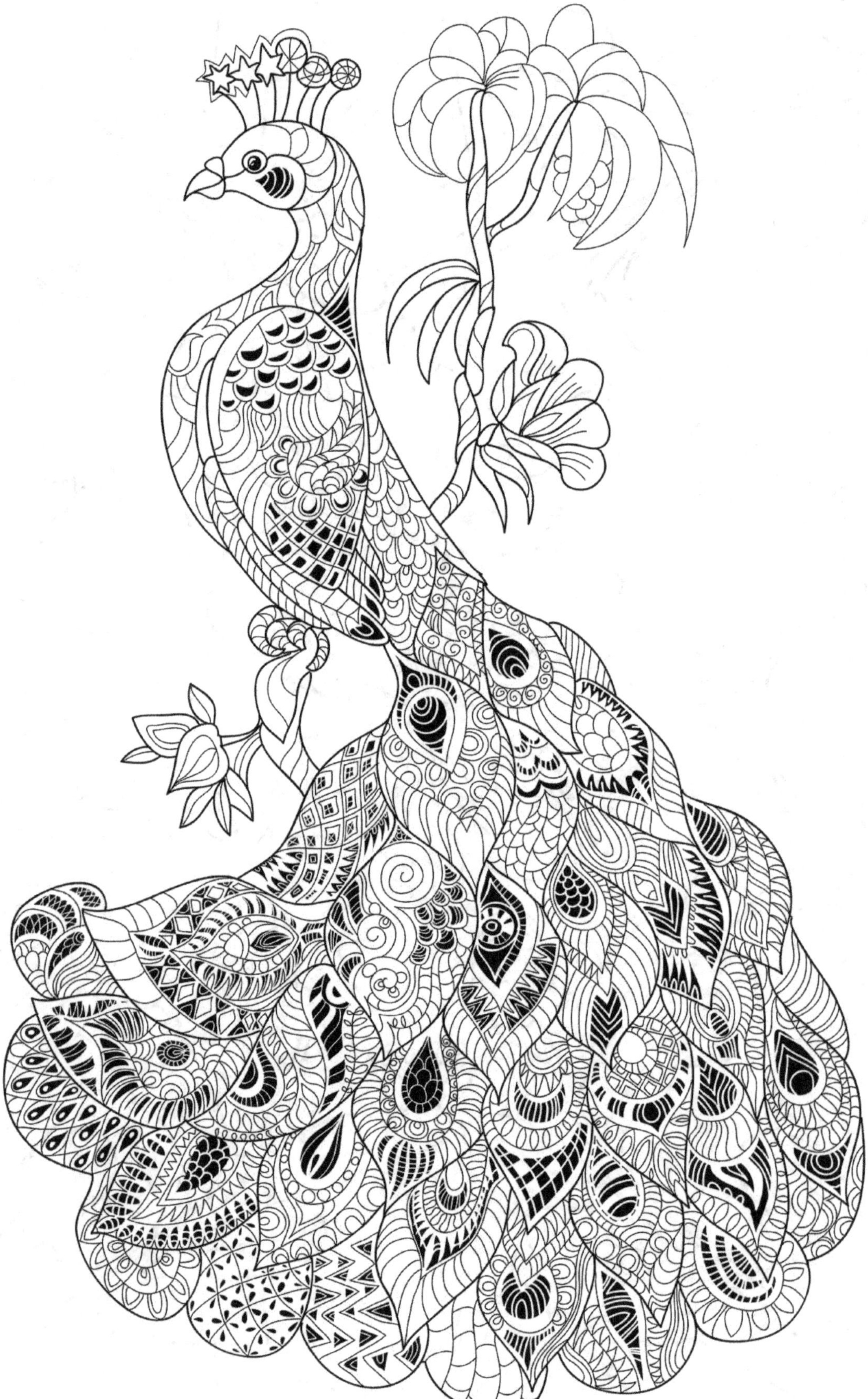

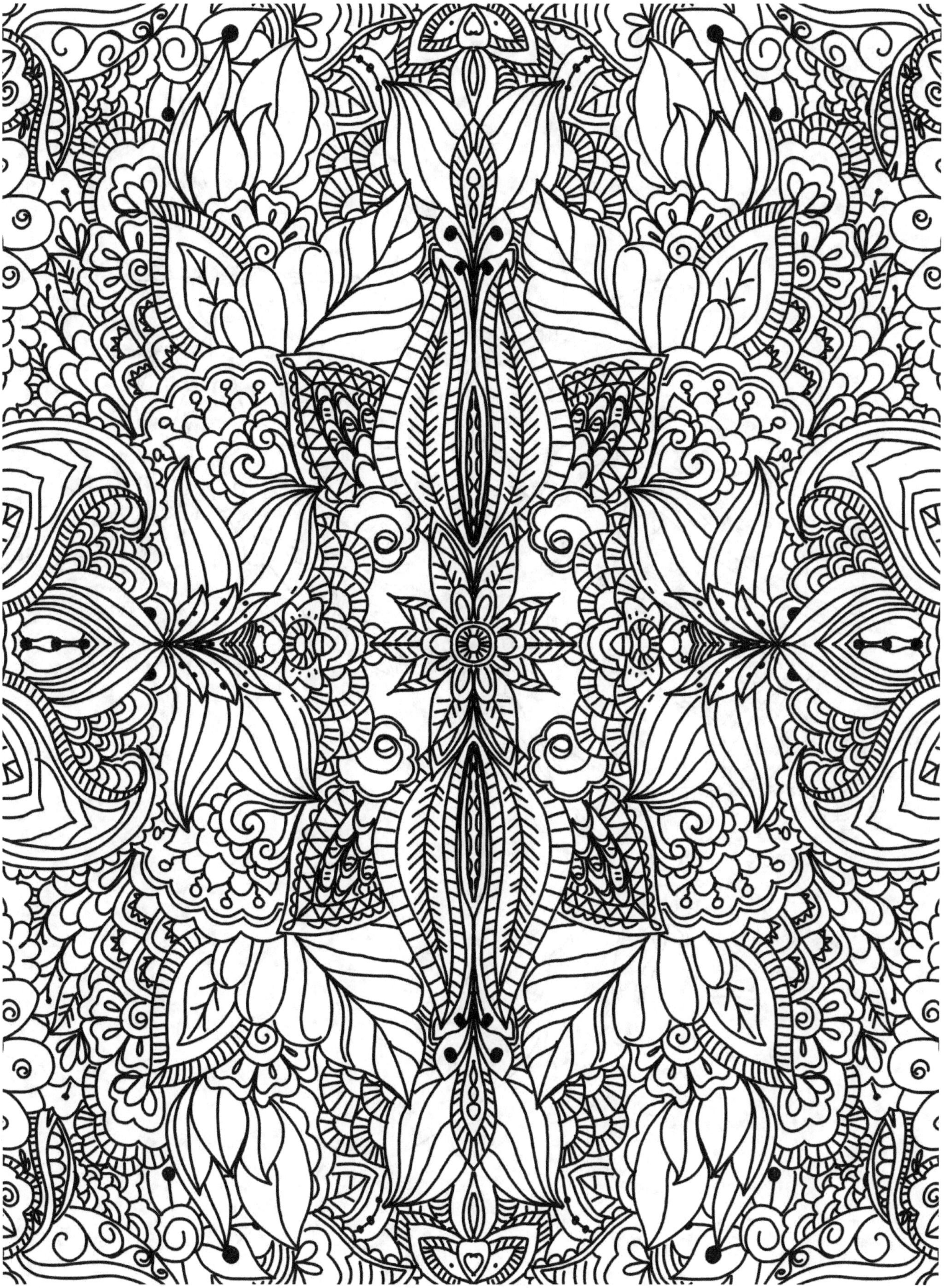

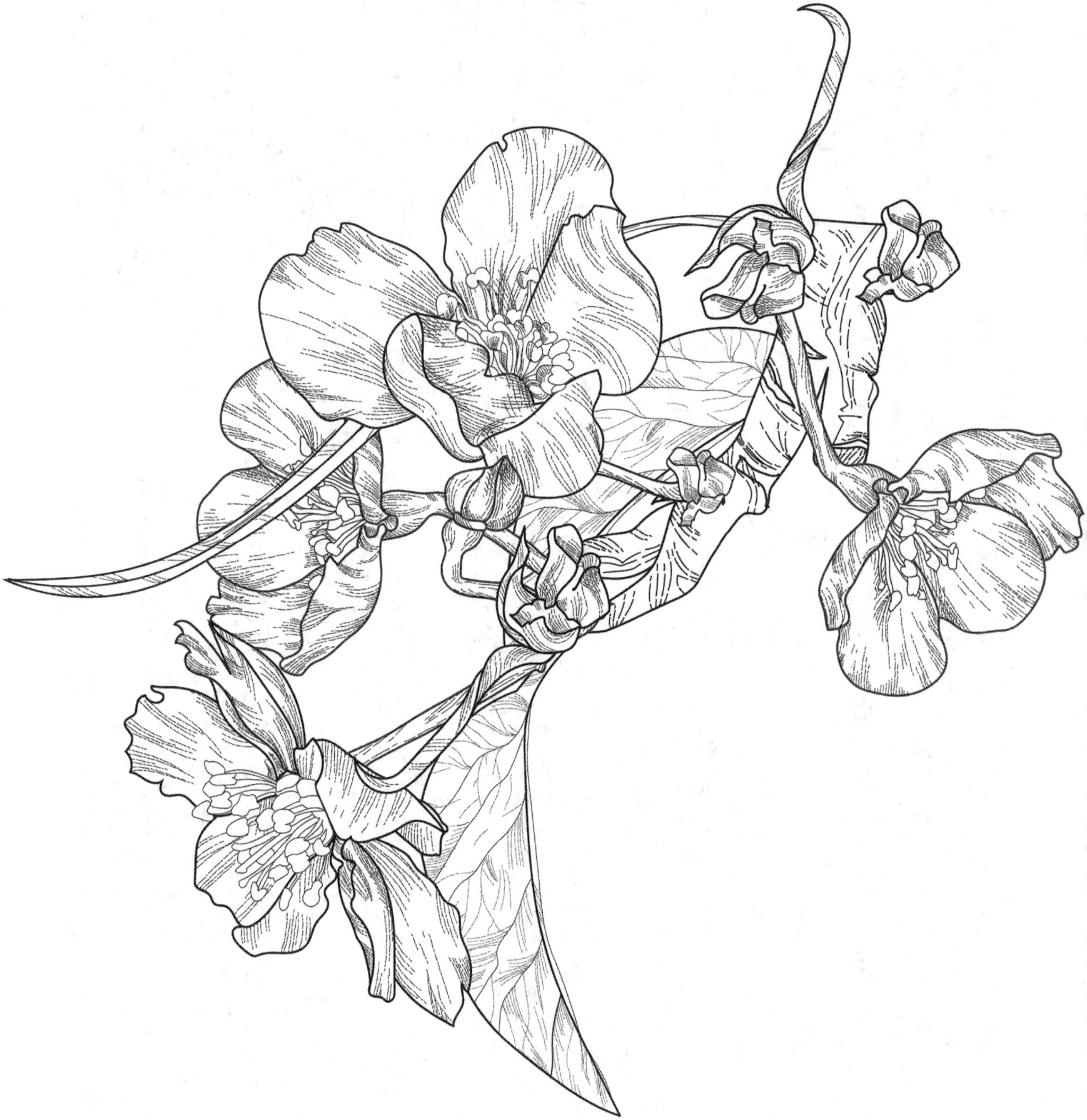

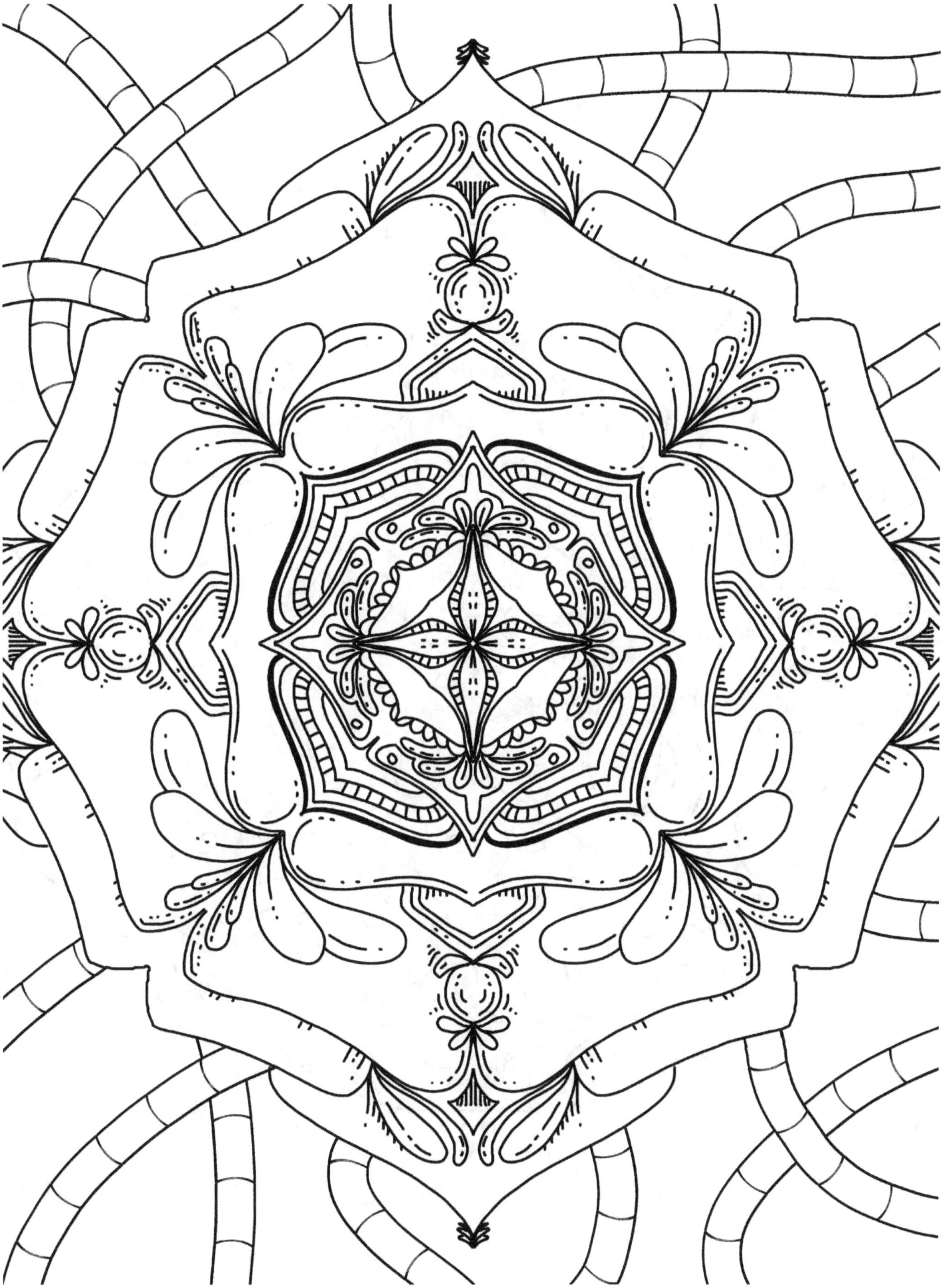

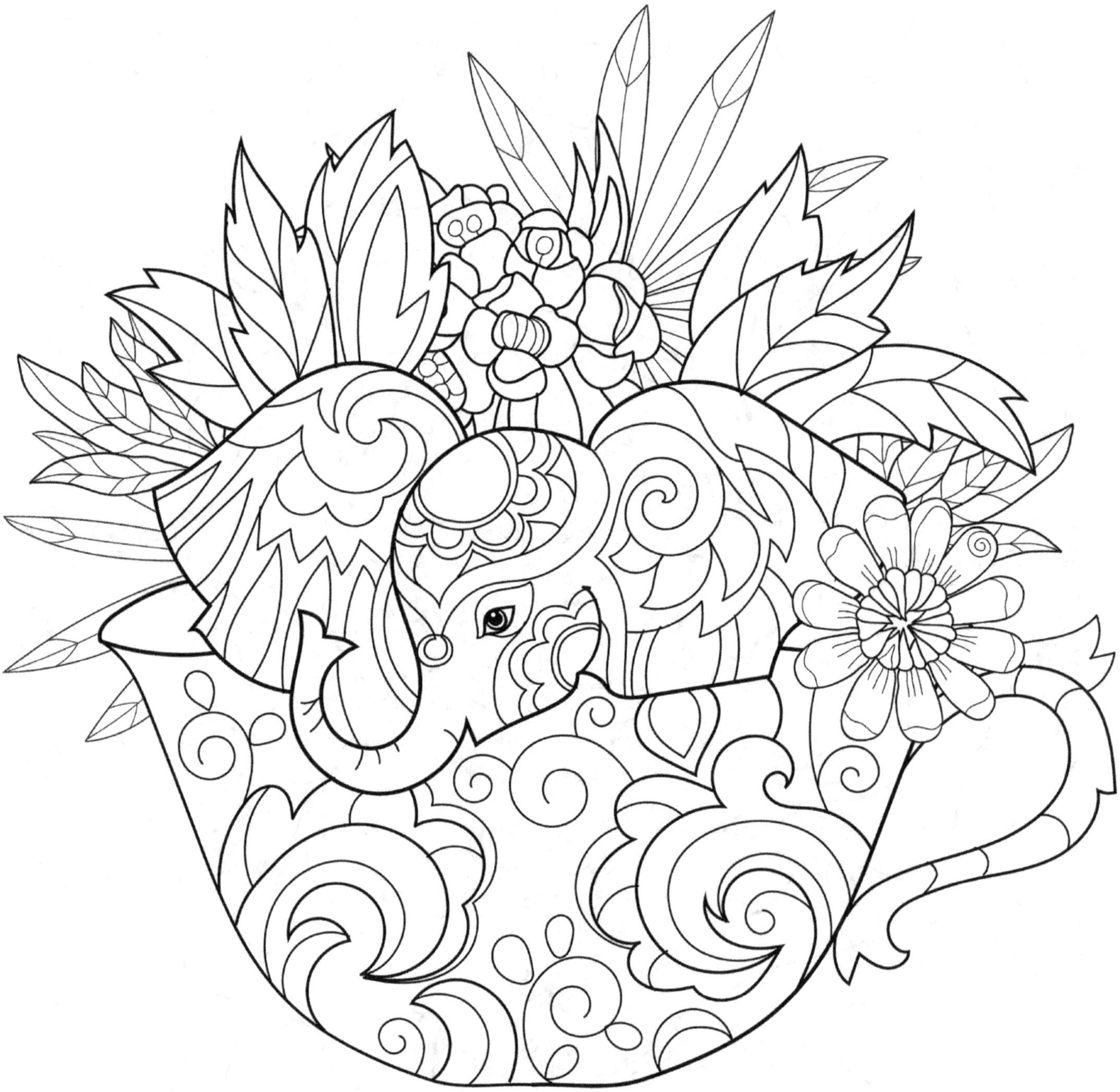

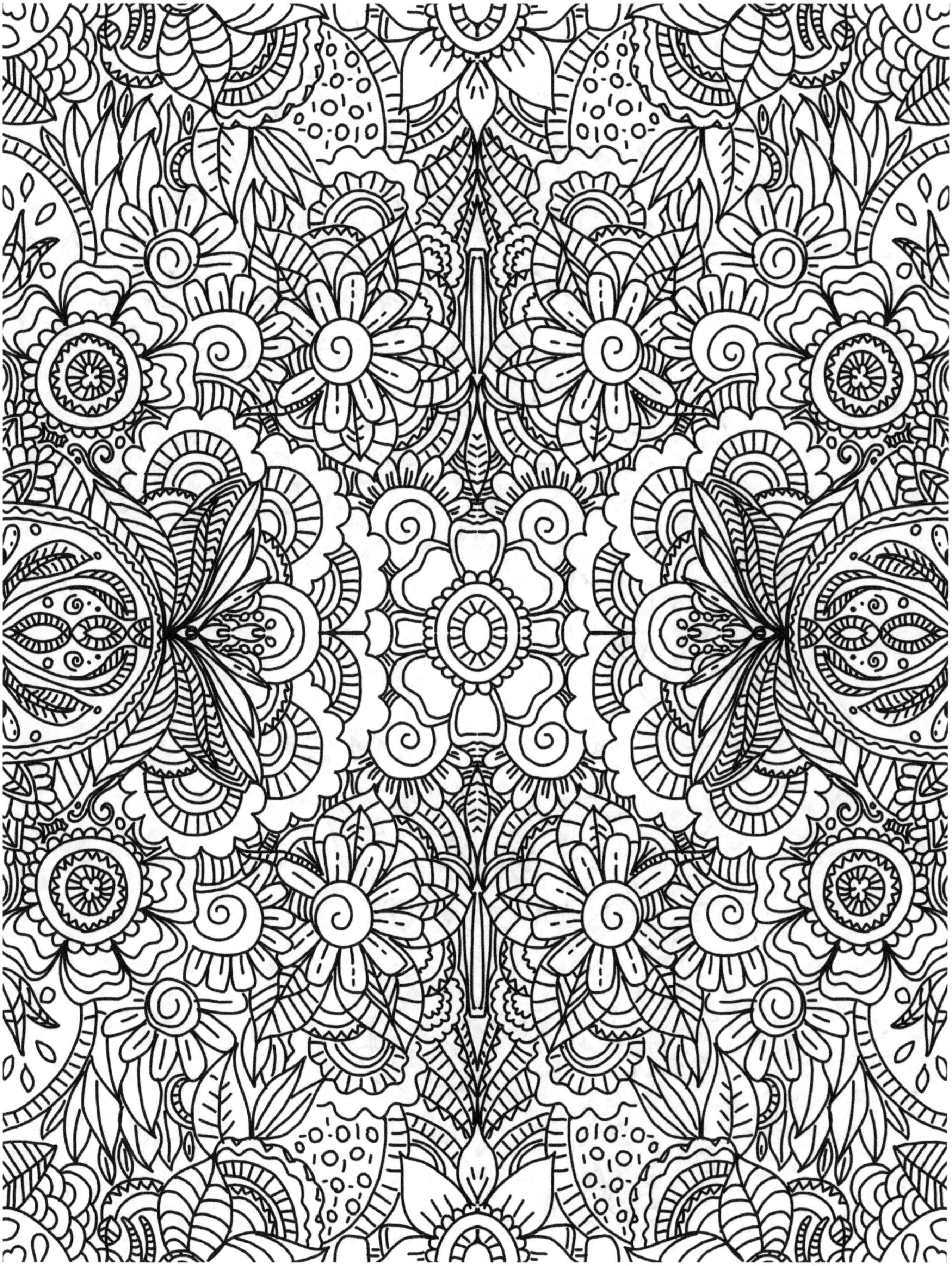

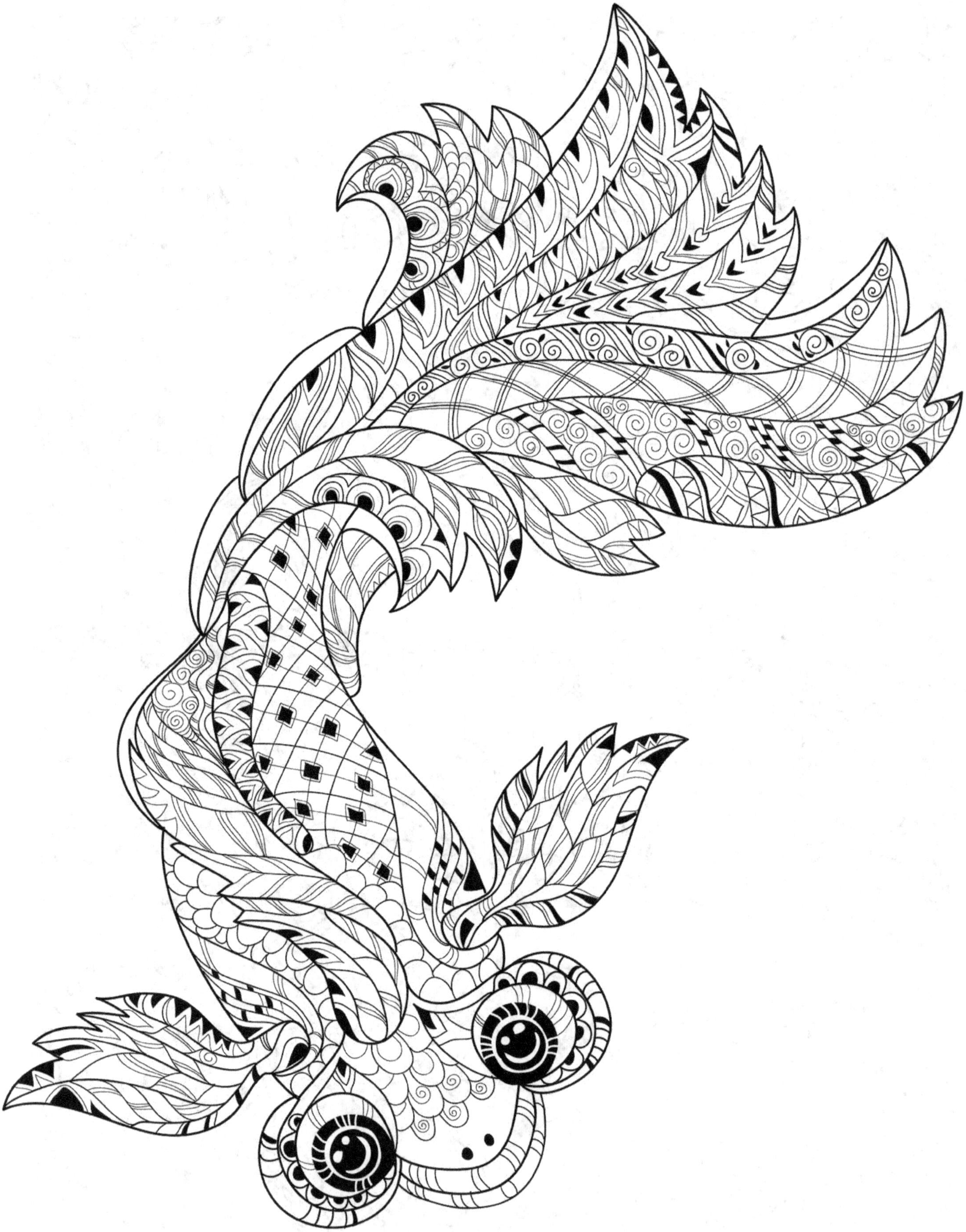

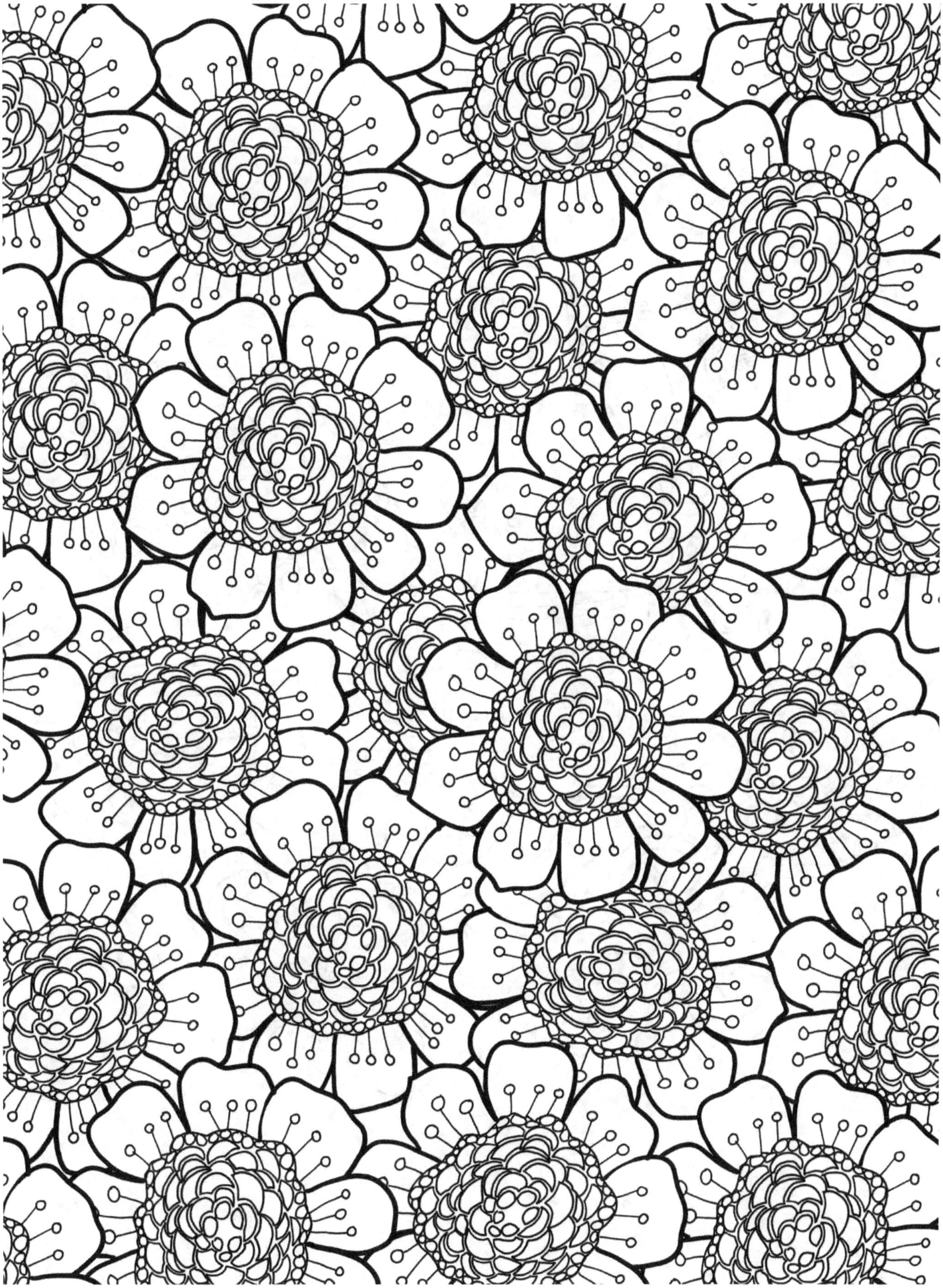

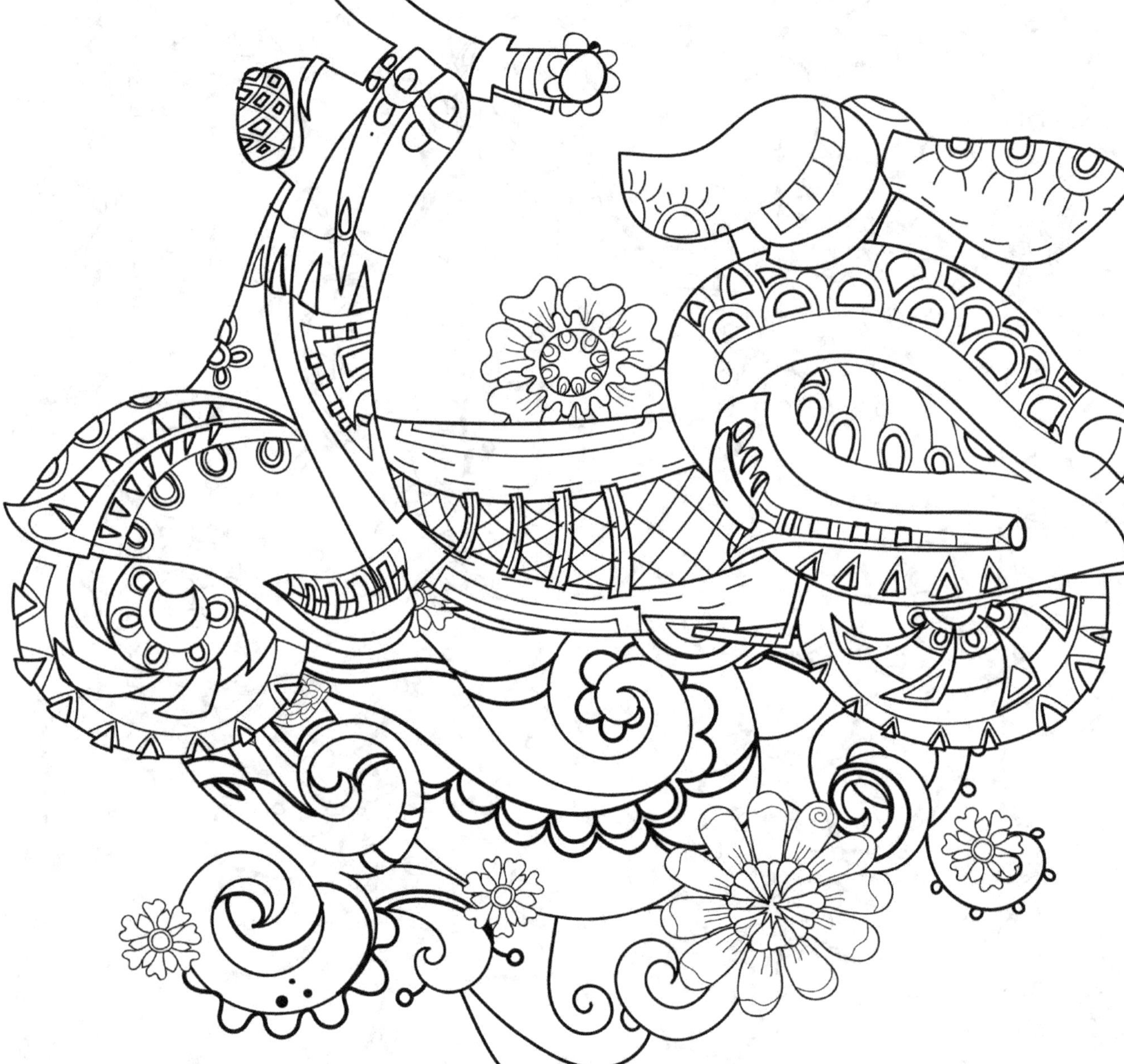

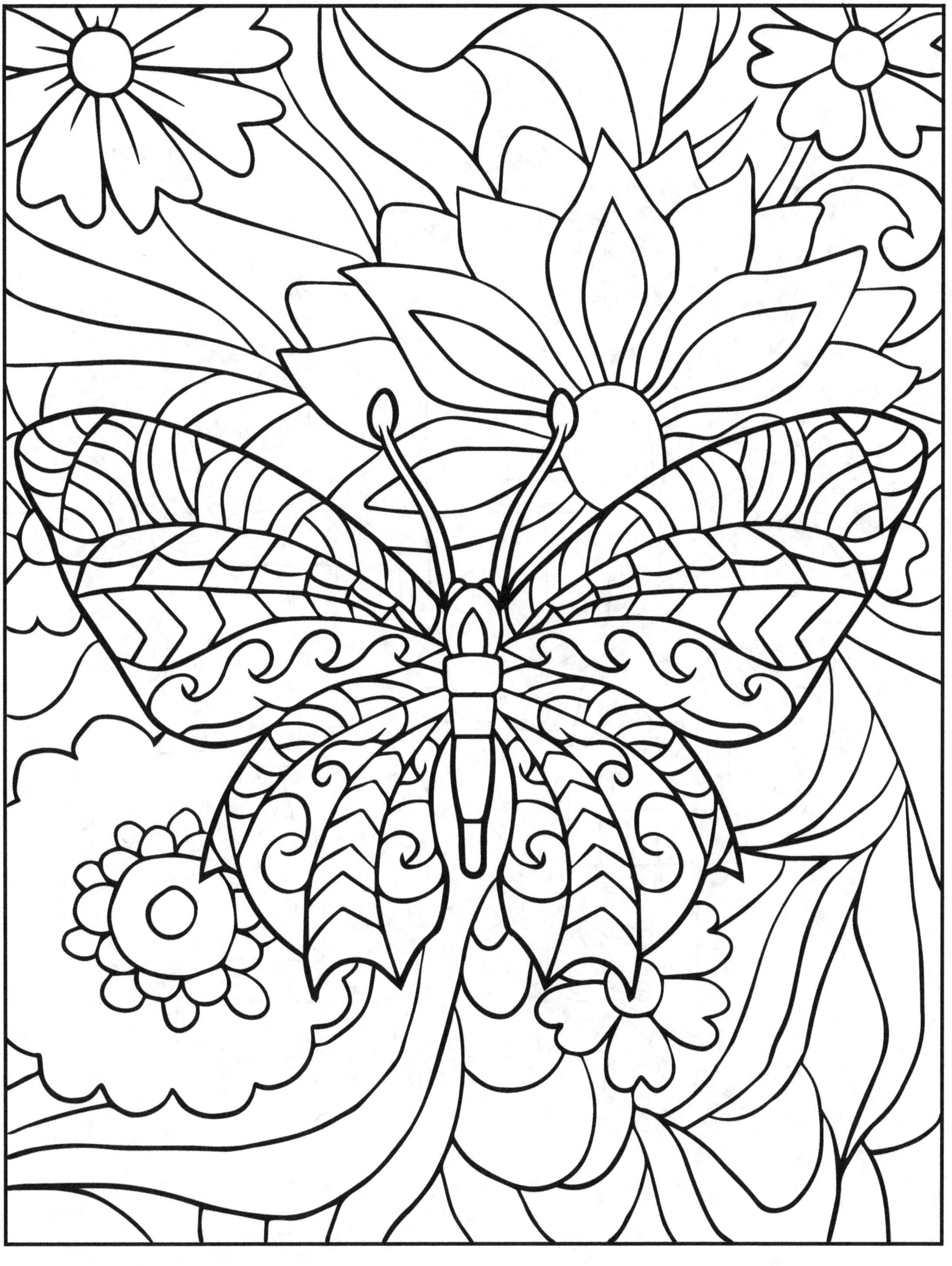

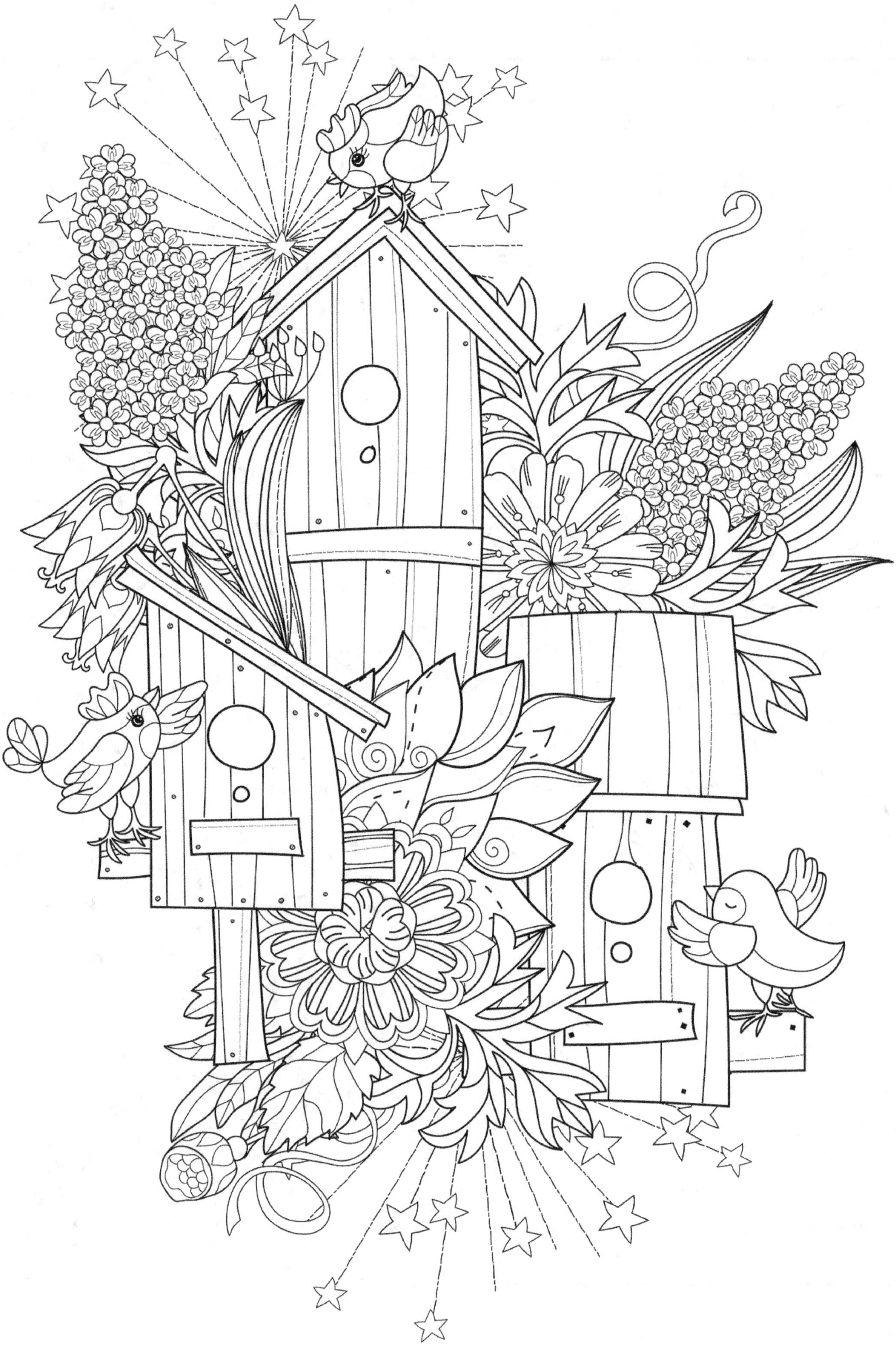

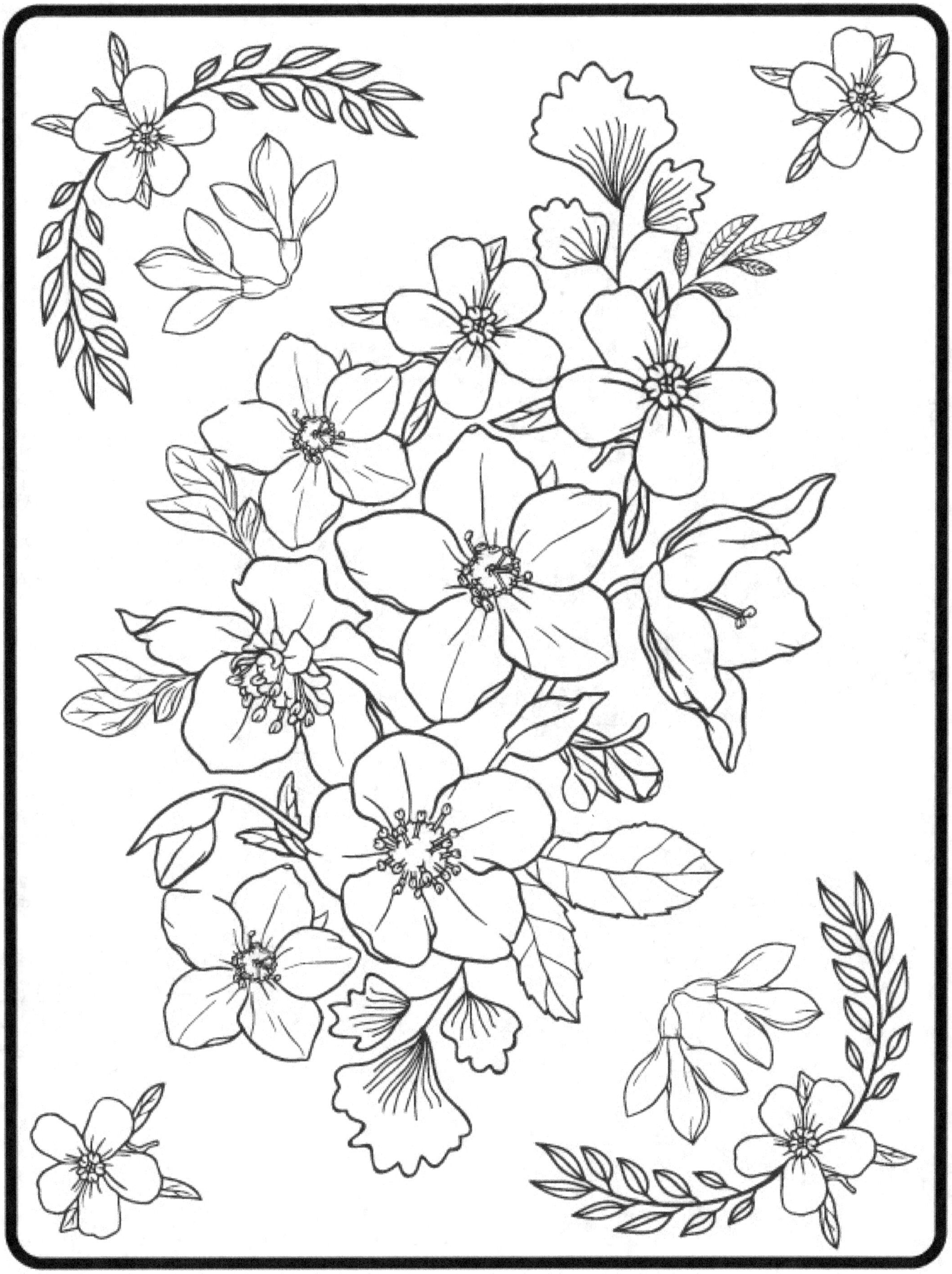

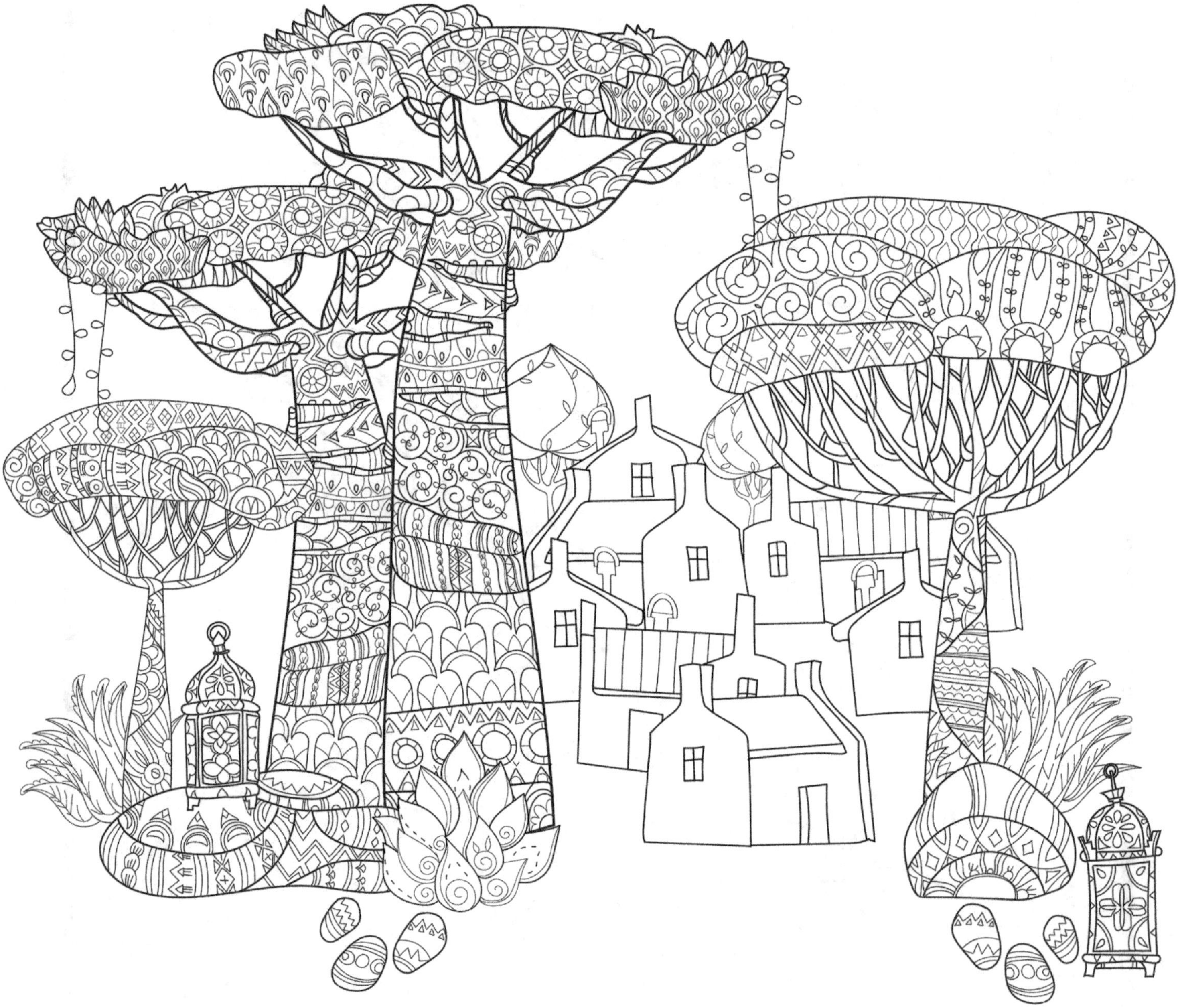

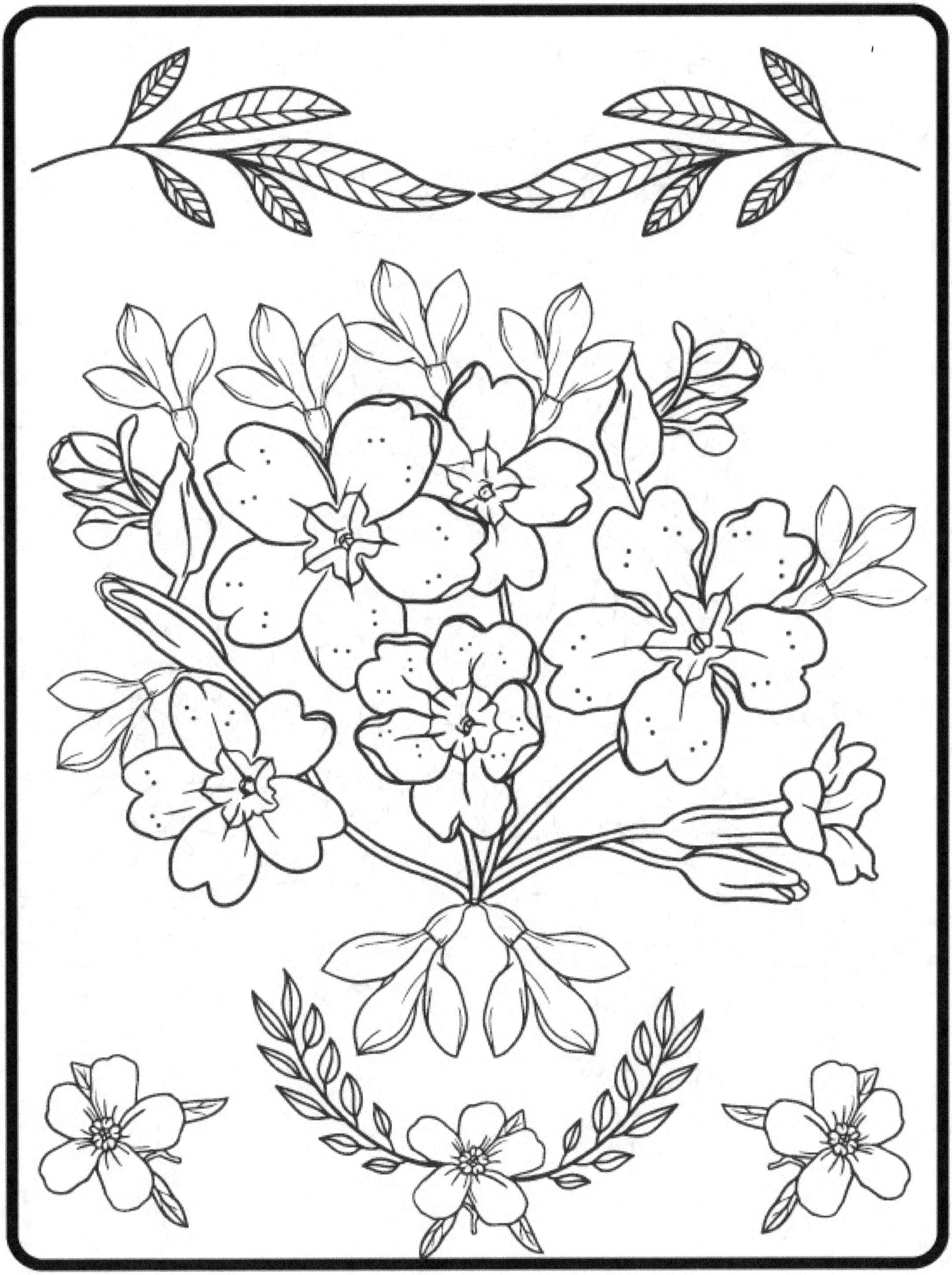

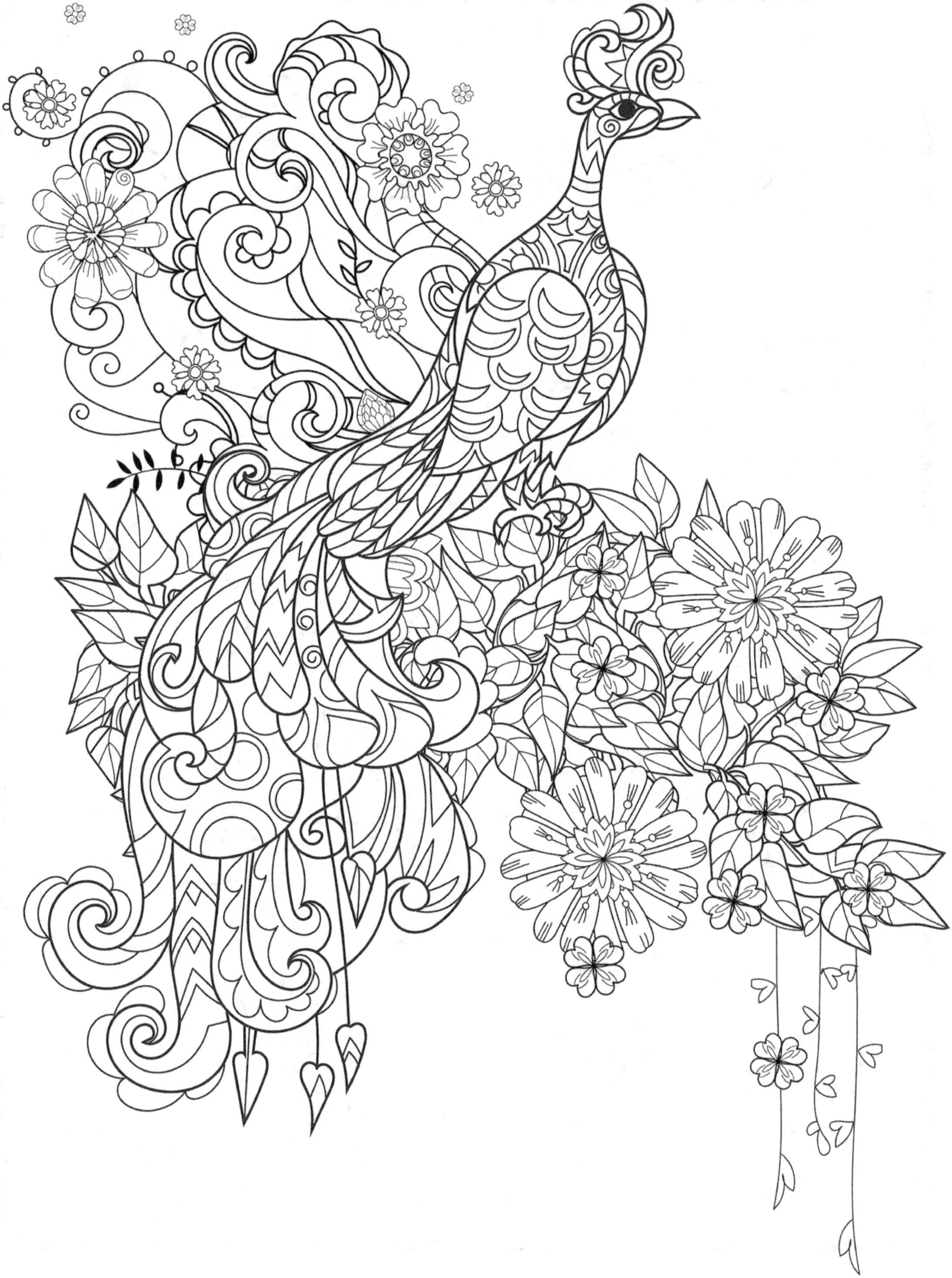

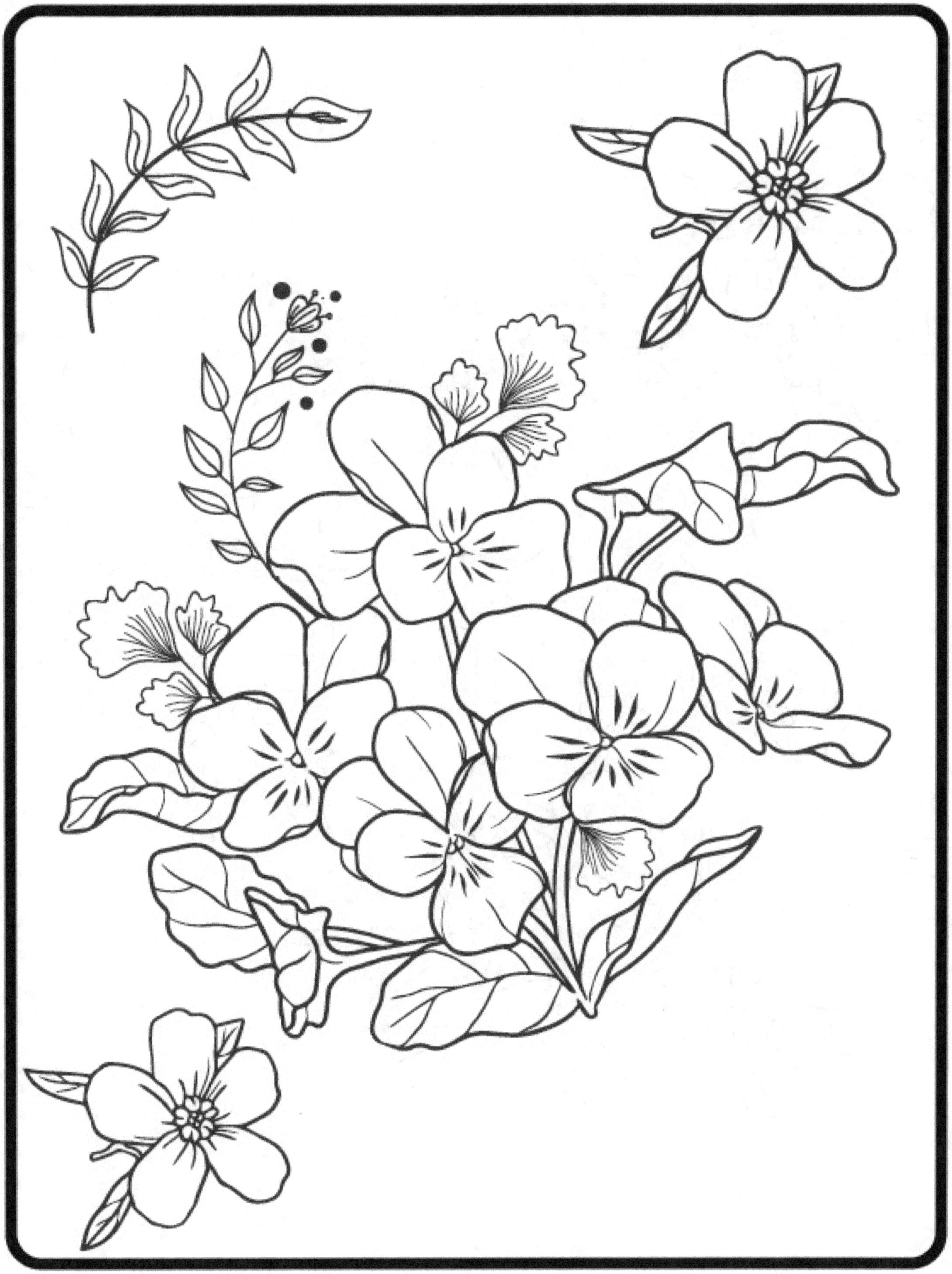

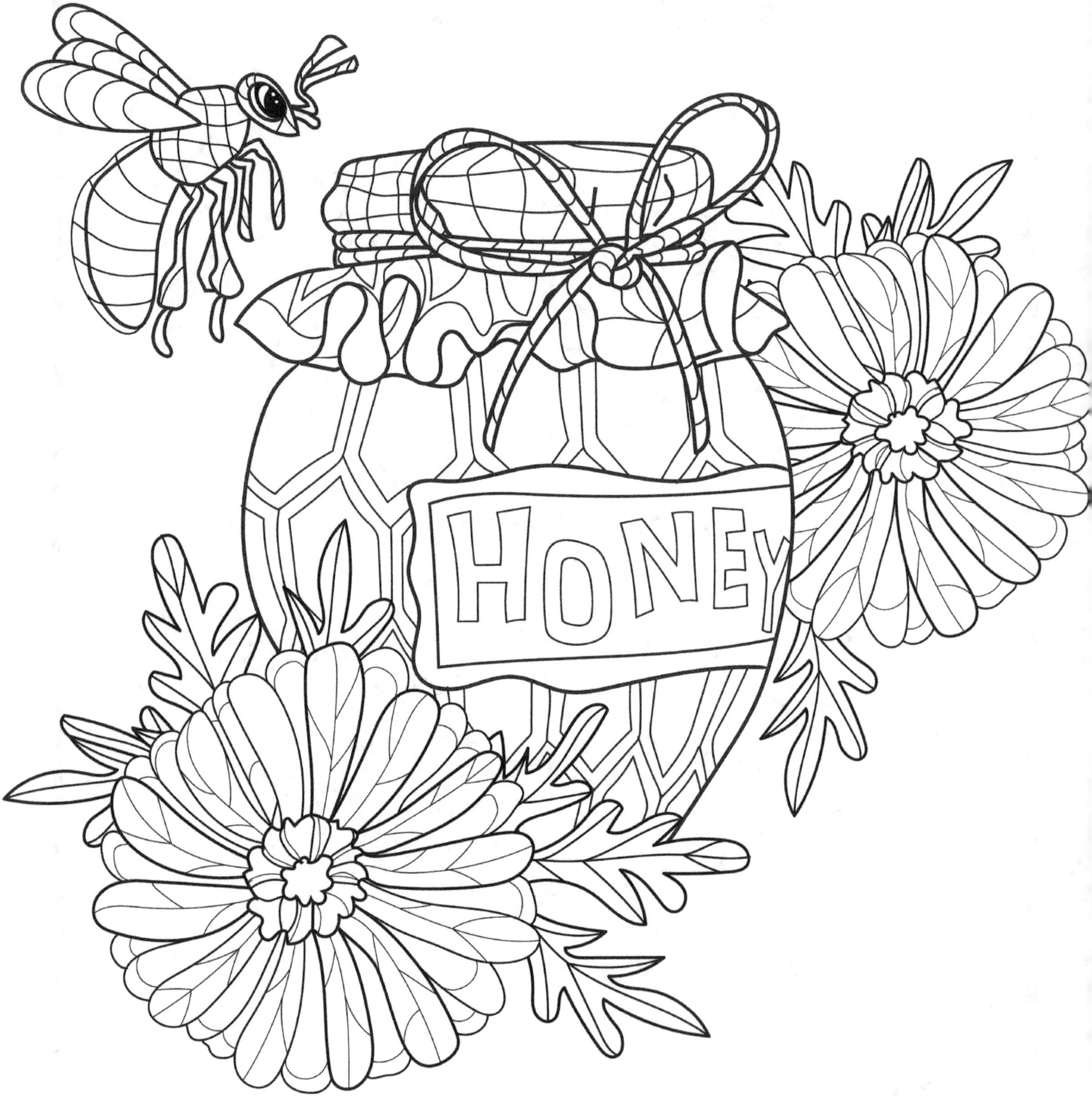
HONEY

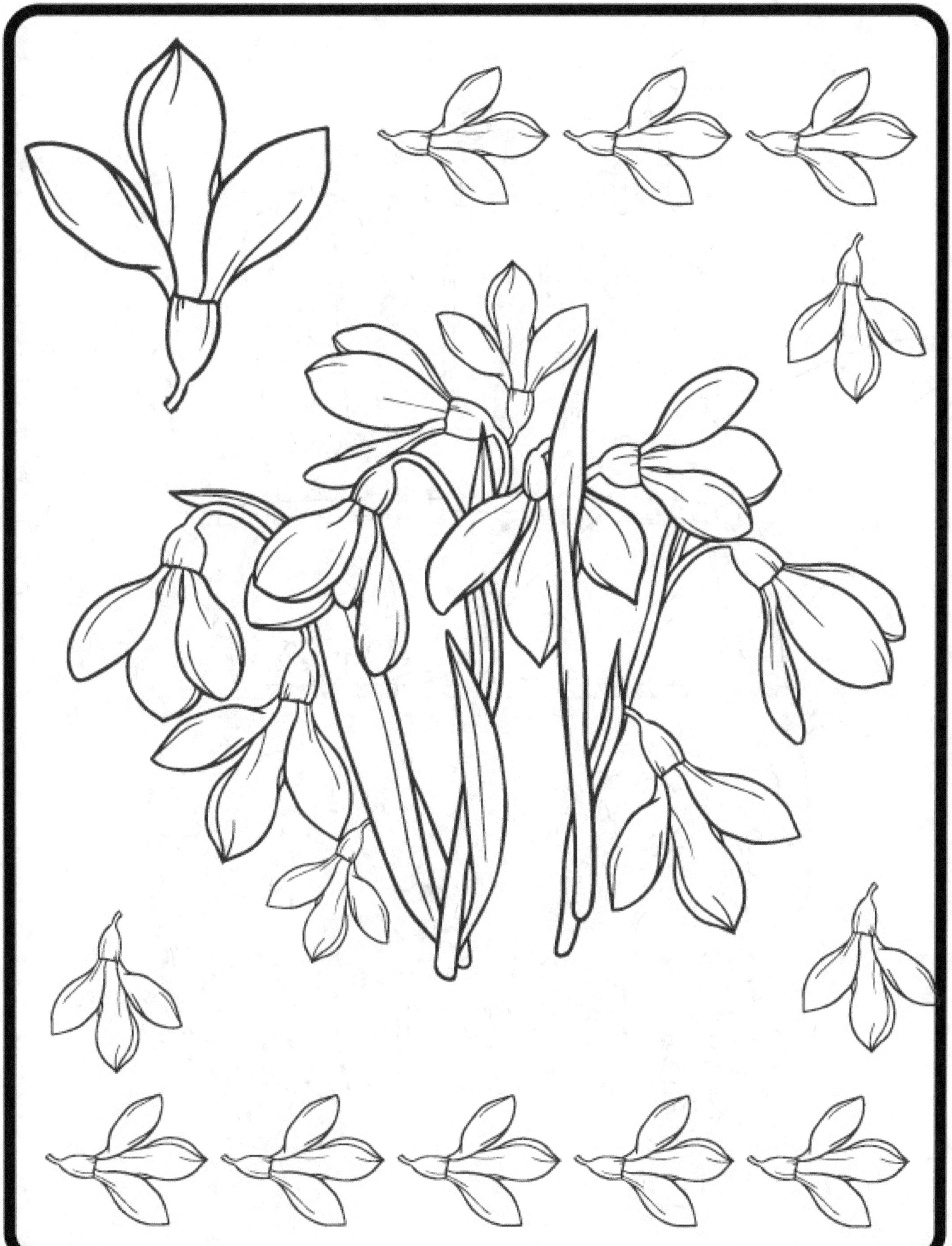

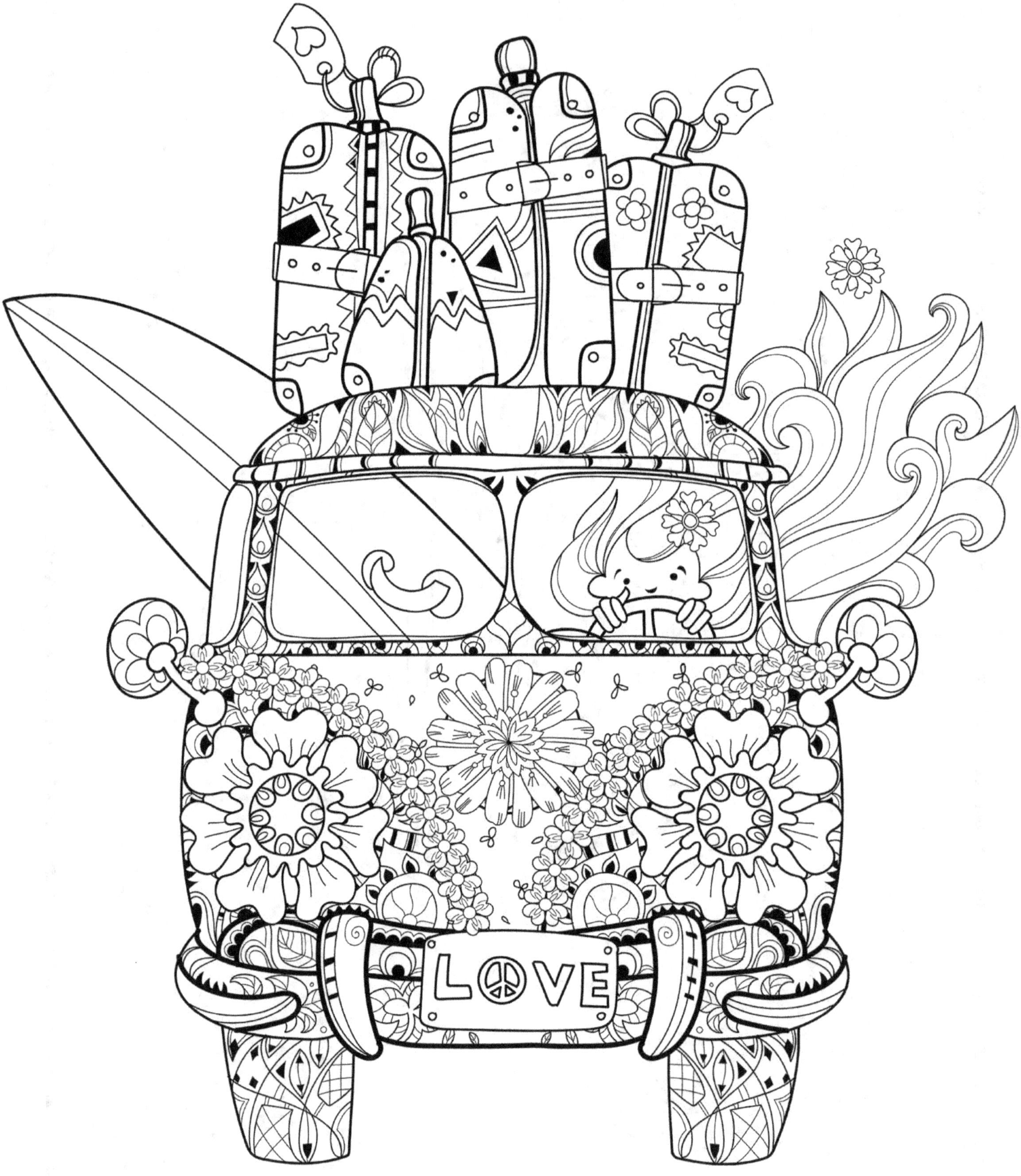
LOVE

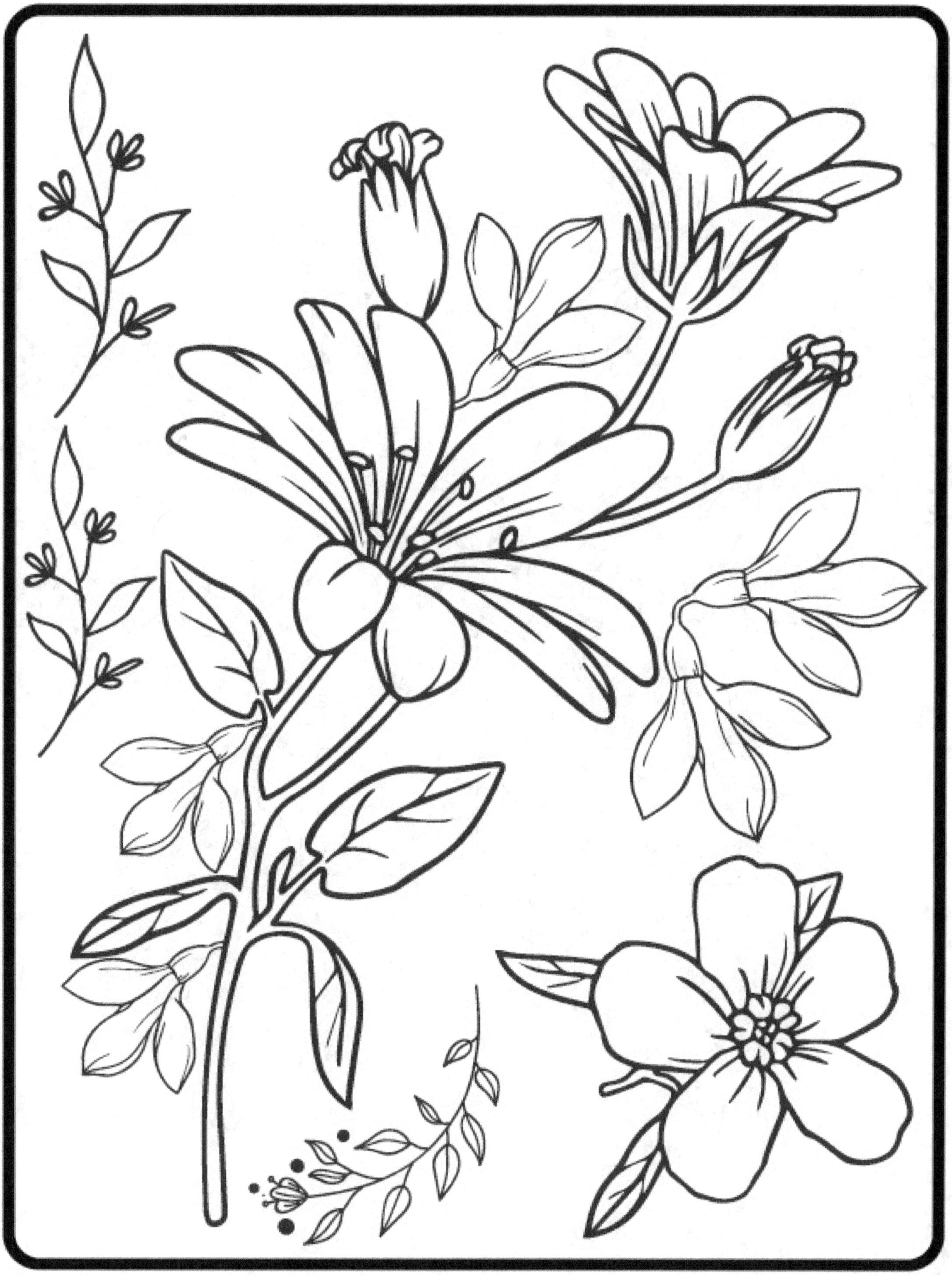

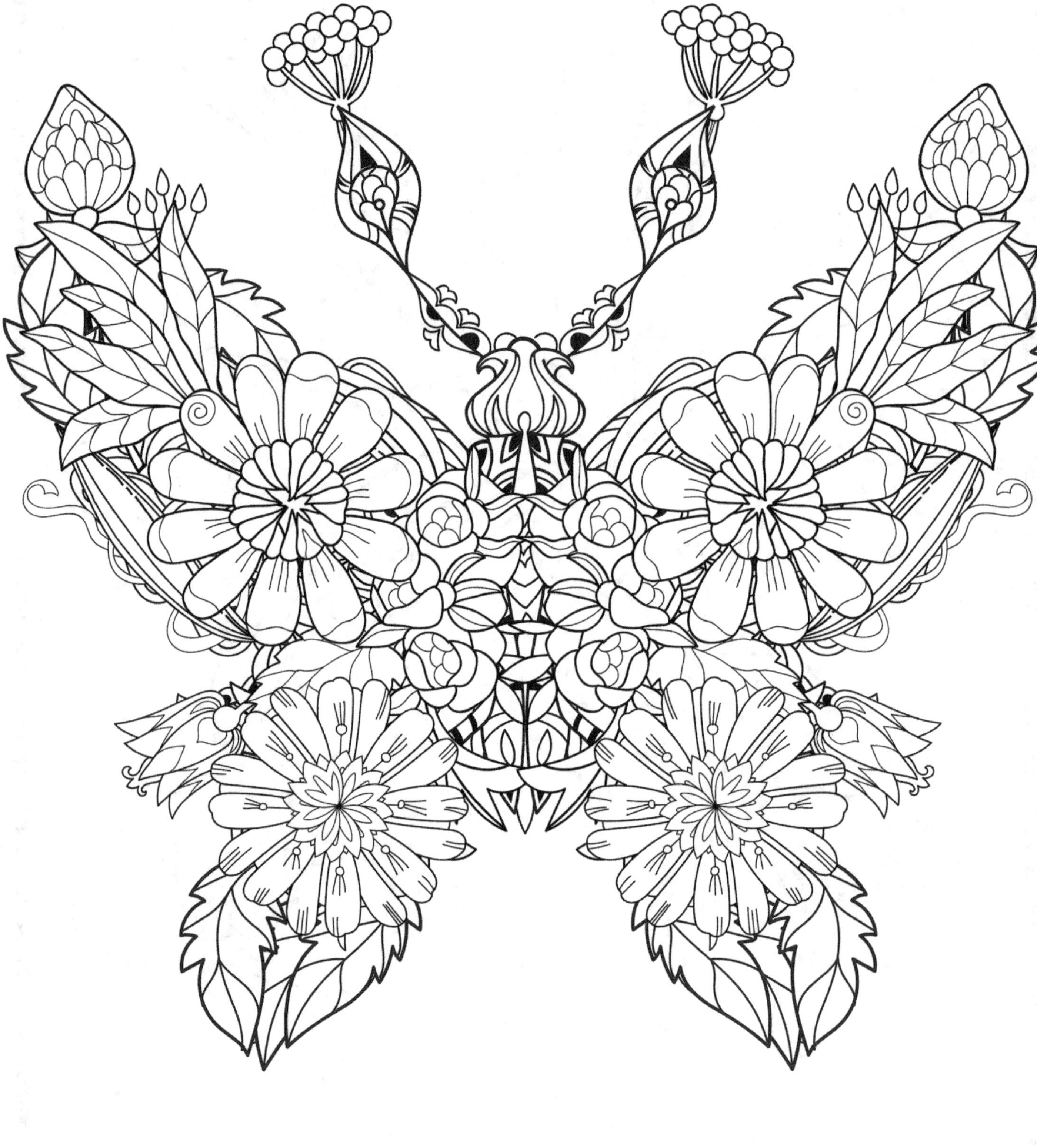

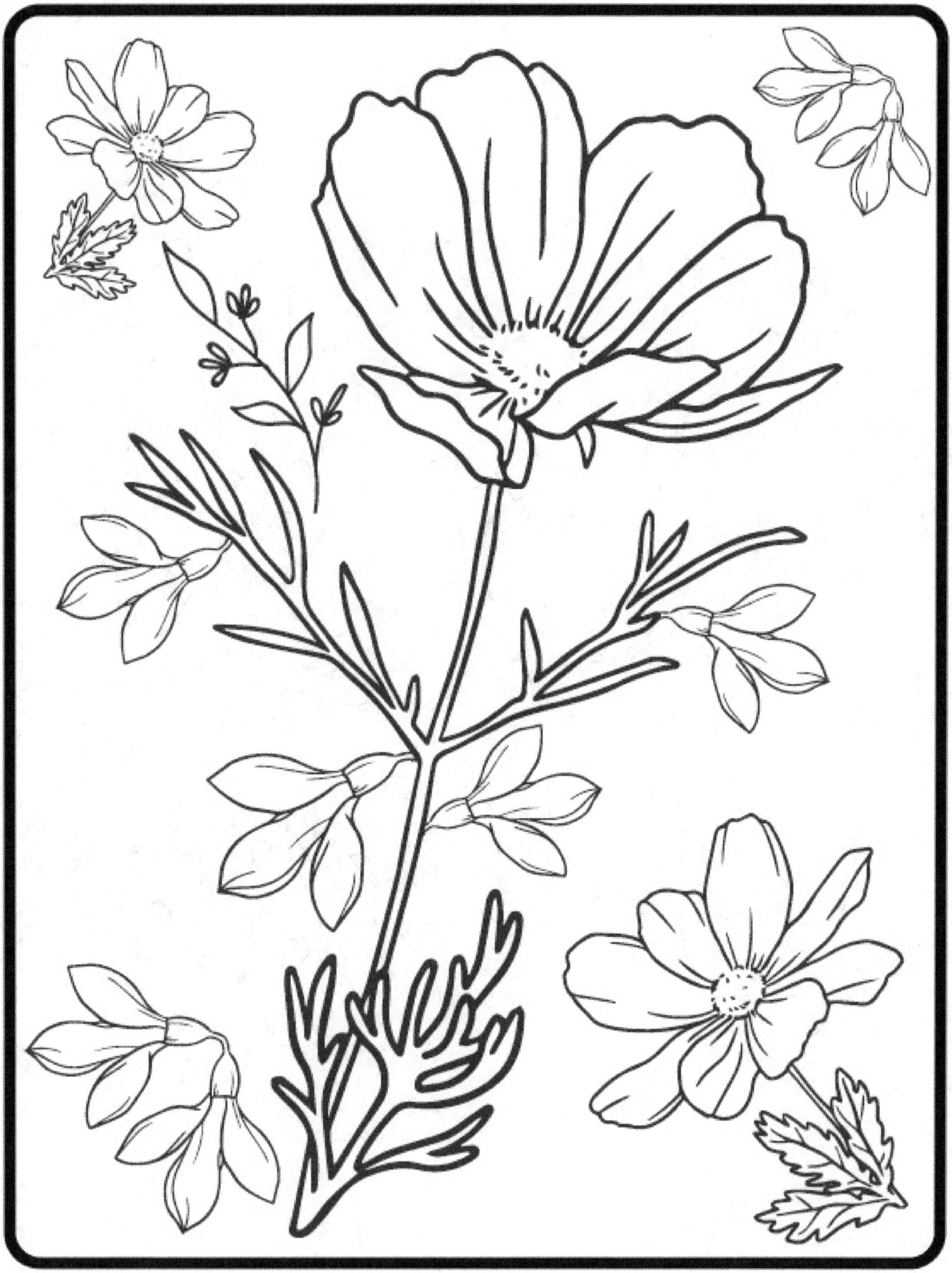

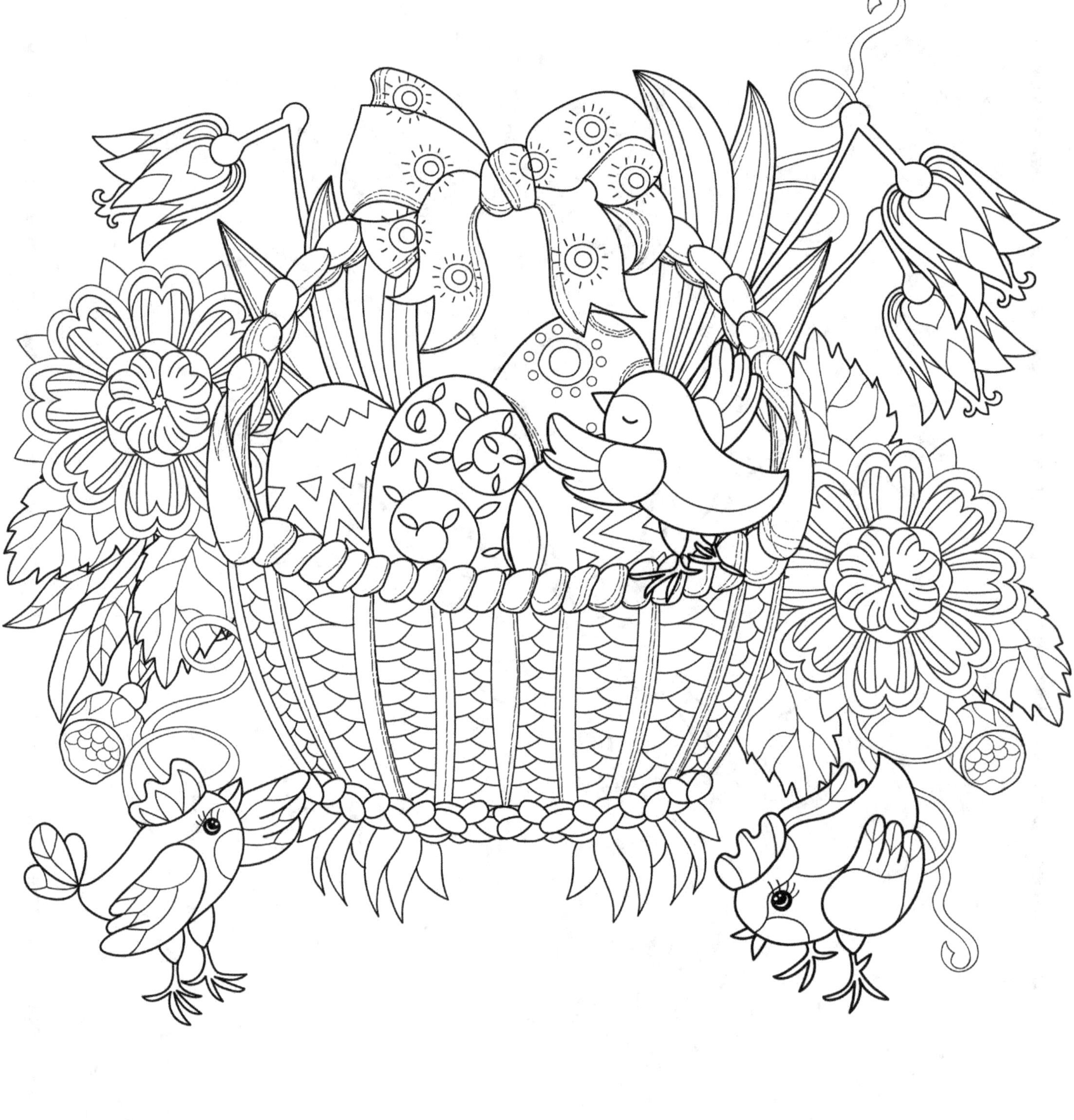

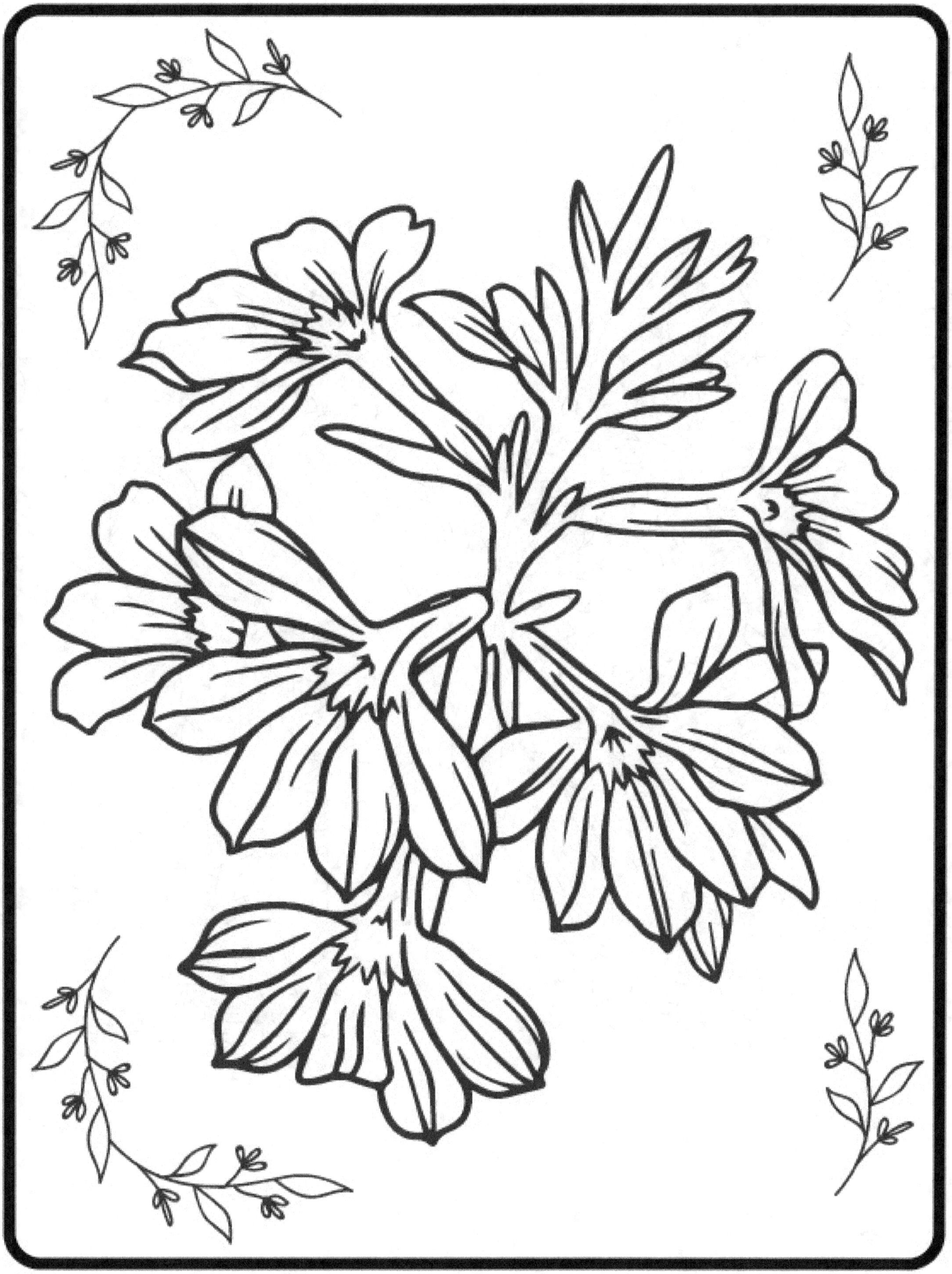

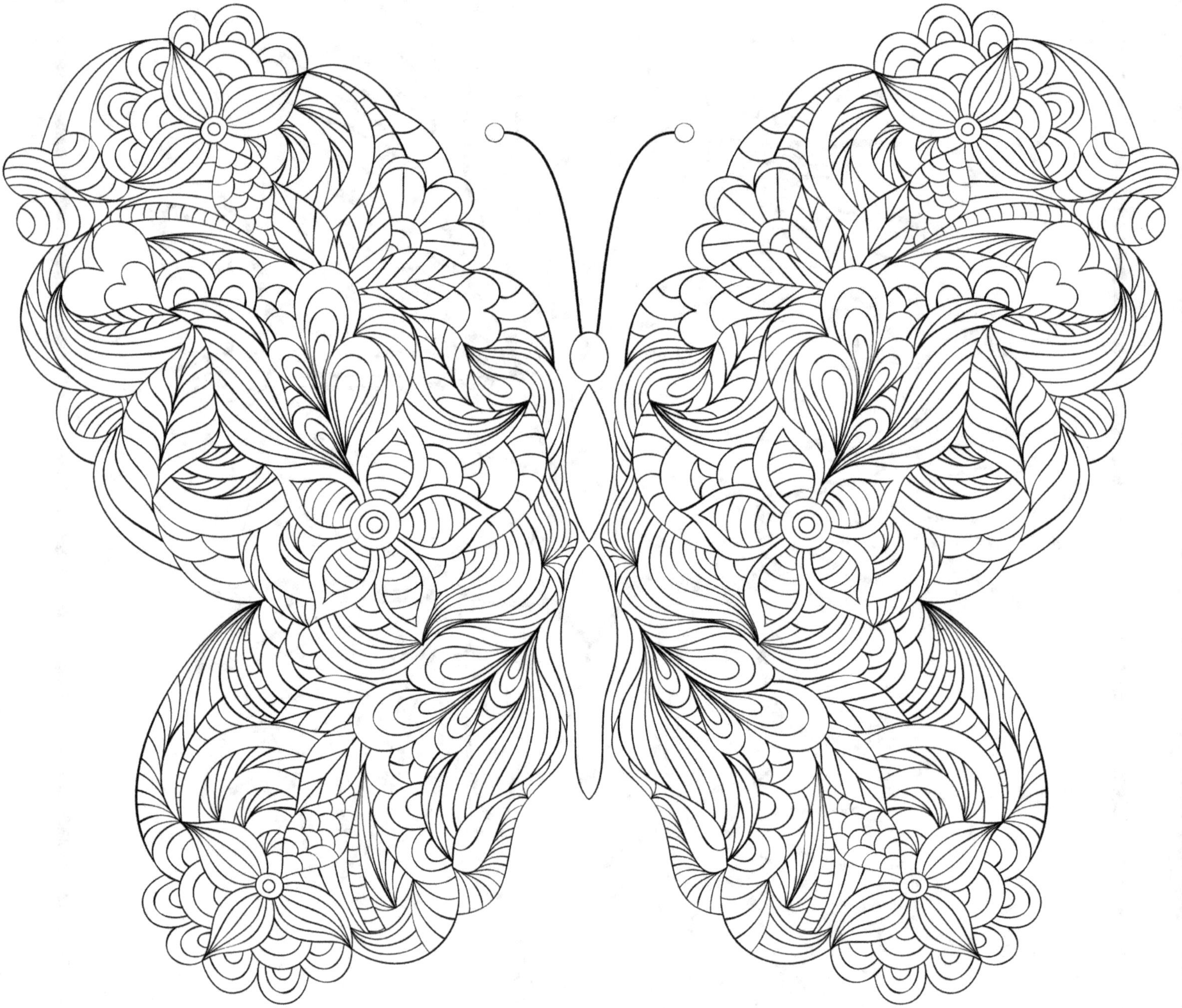

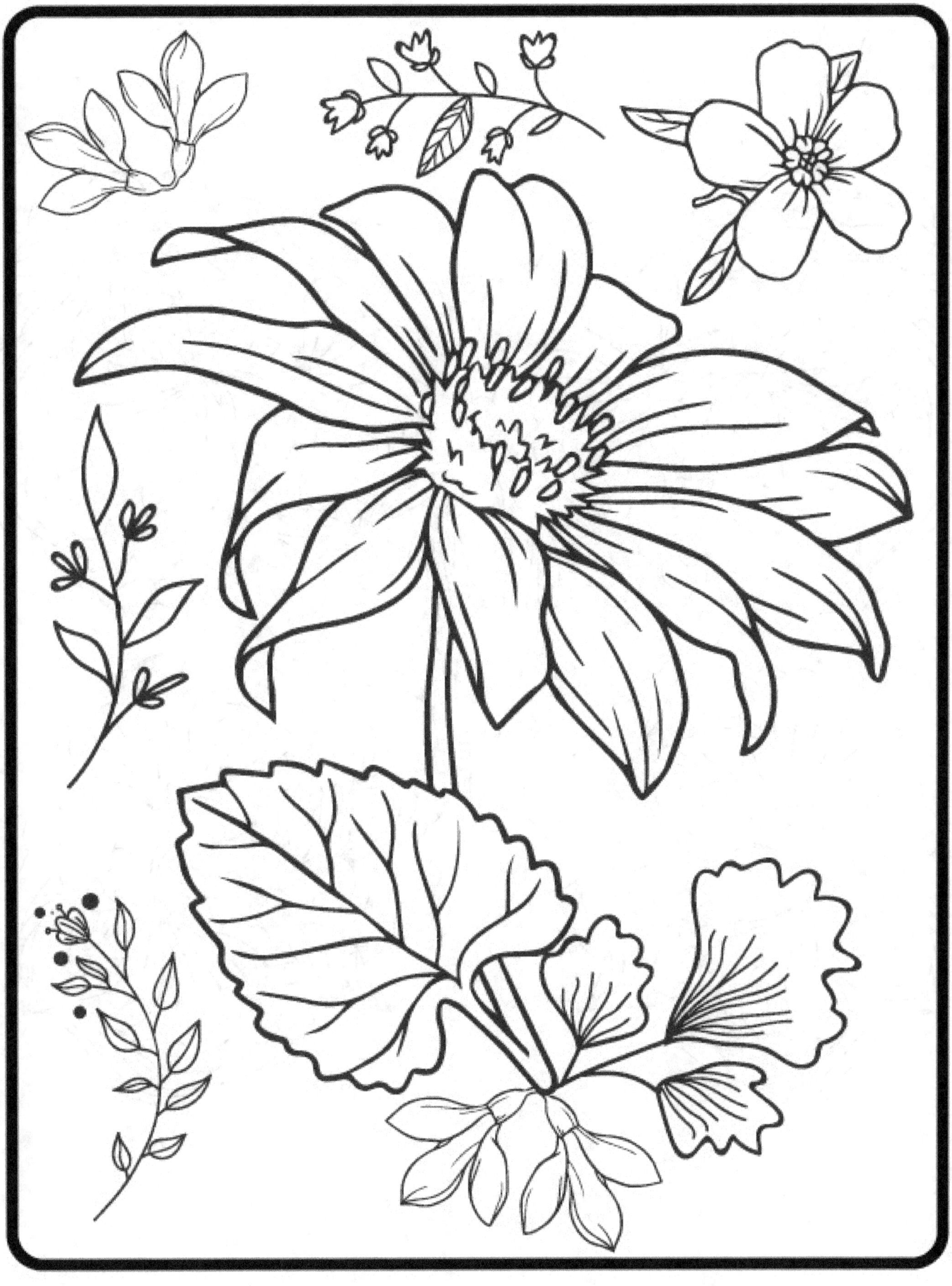

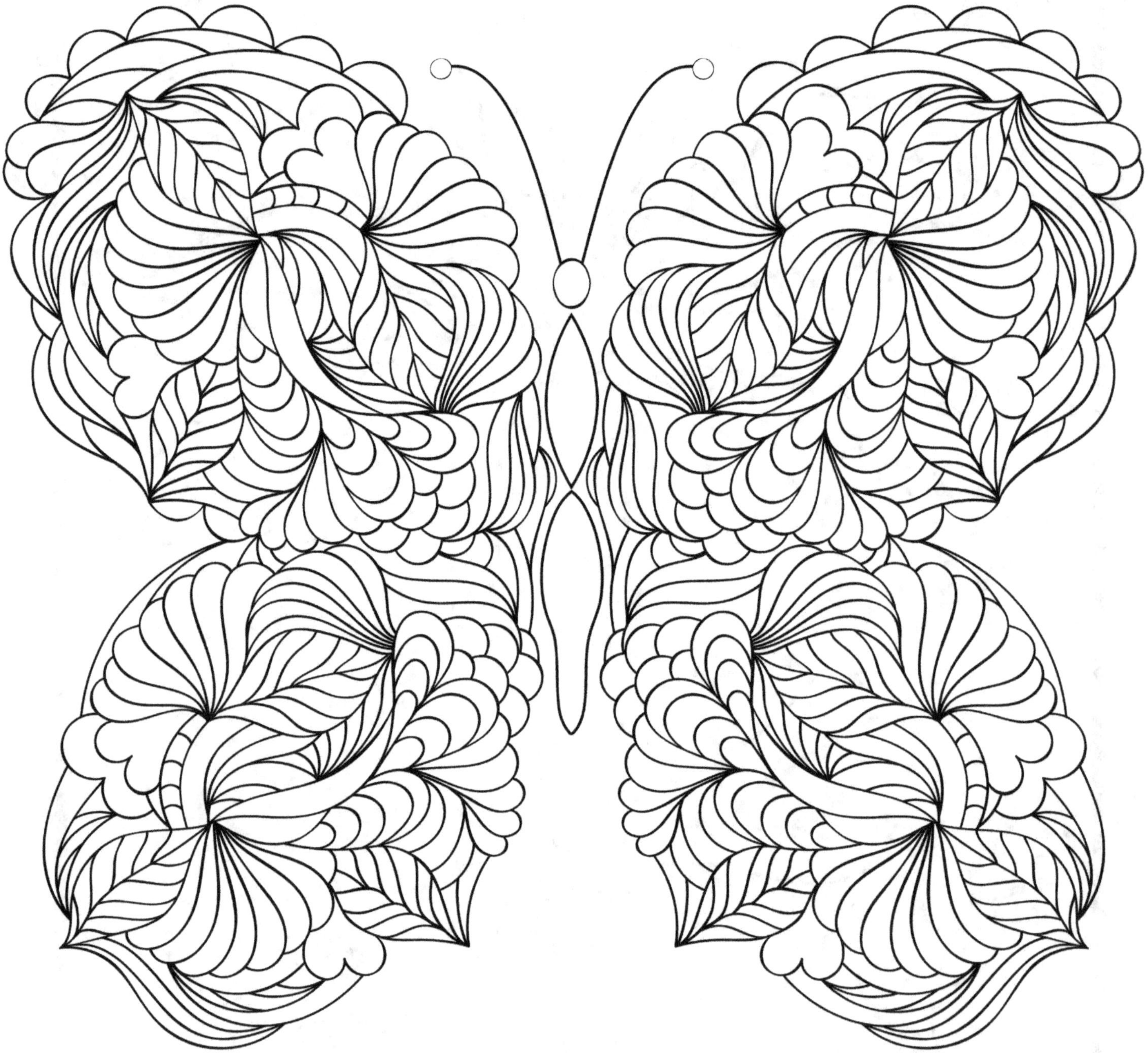

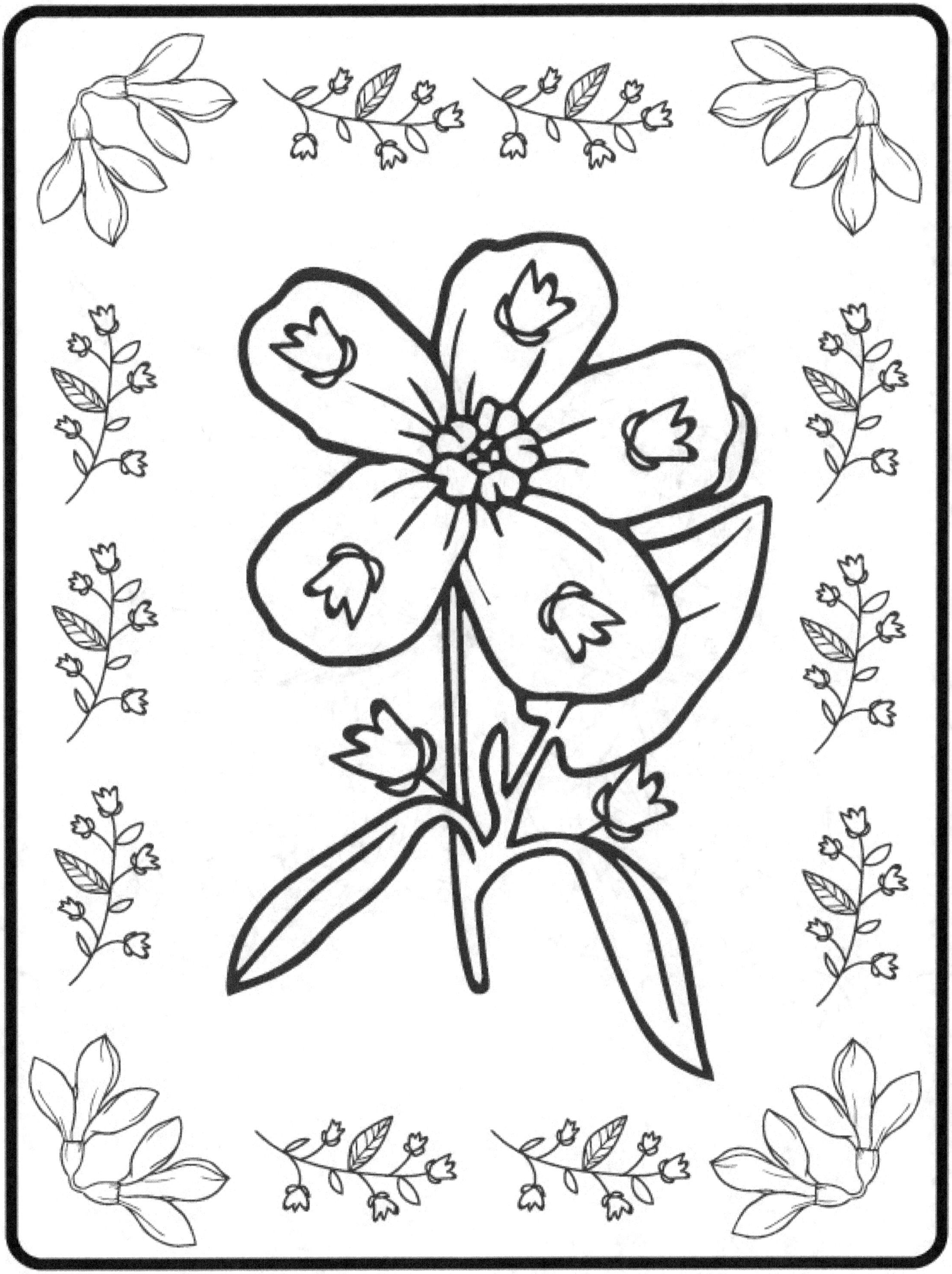

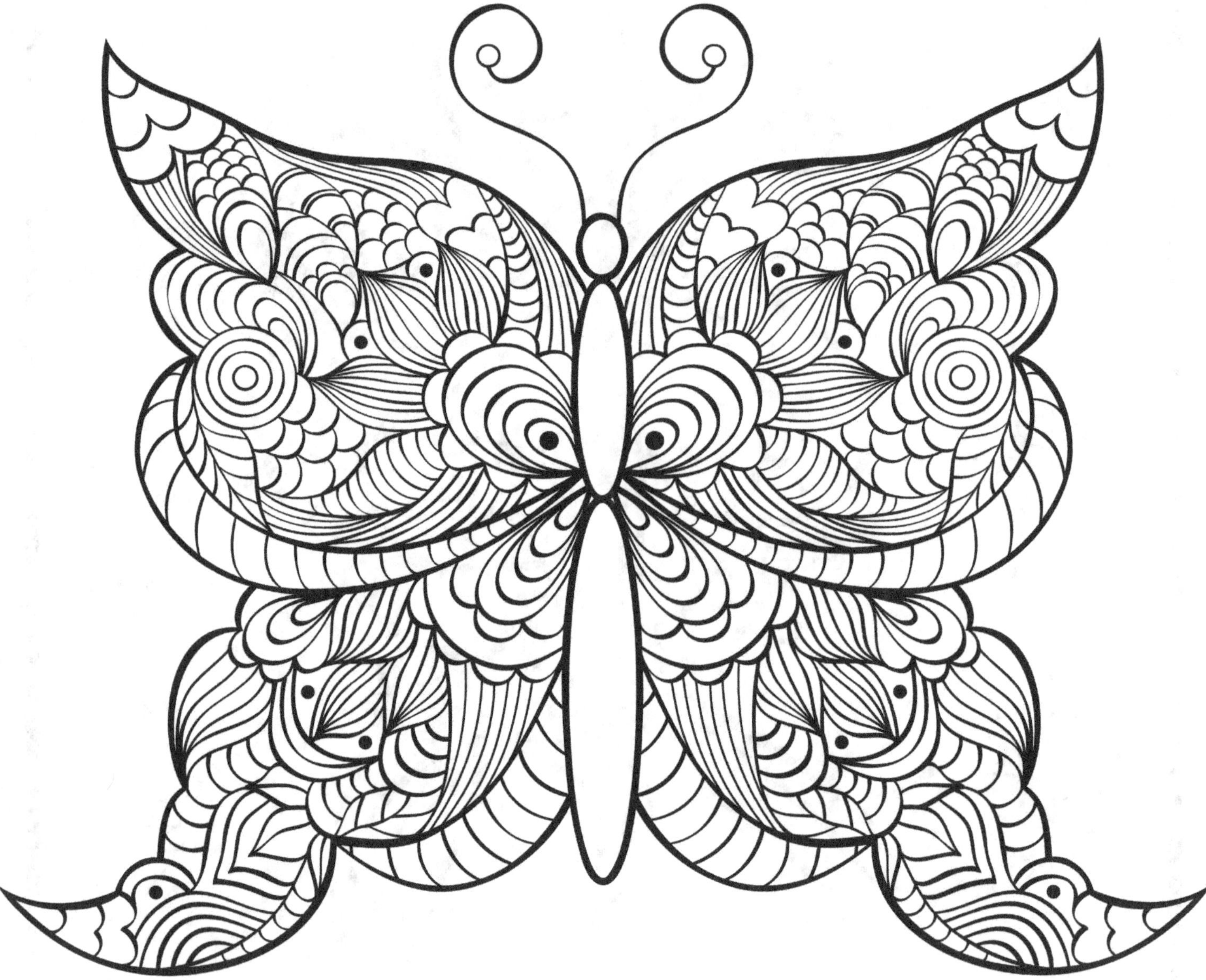

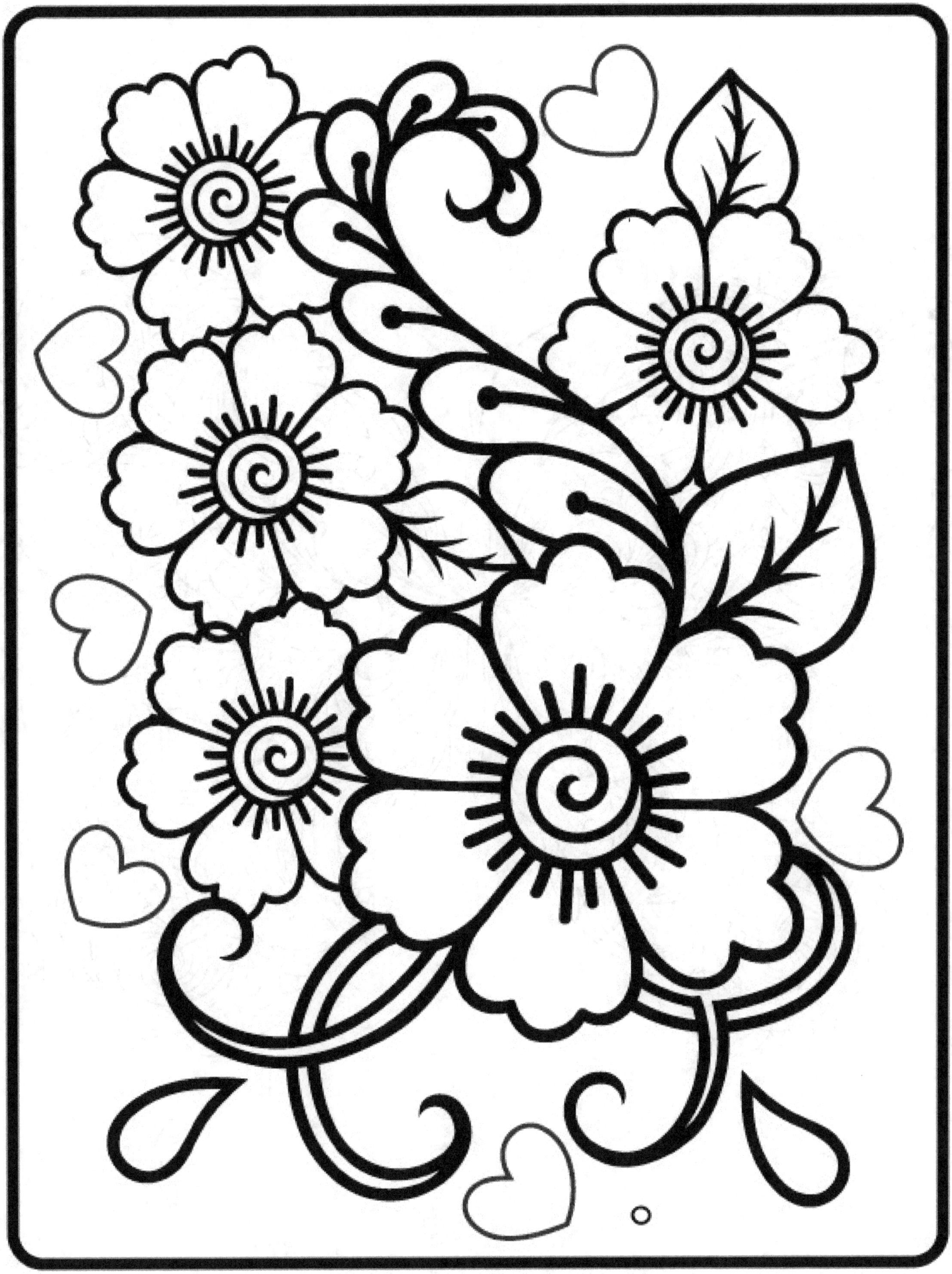

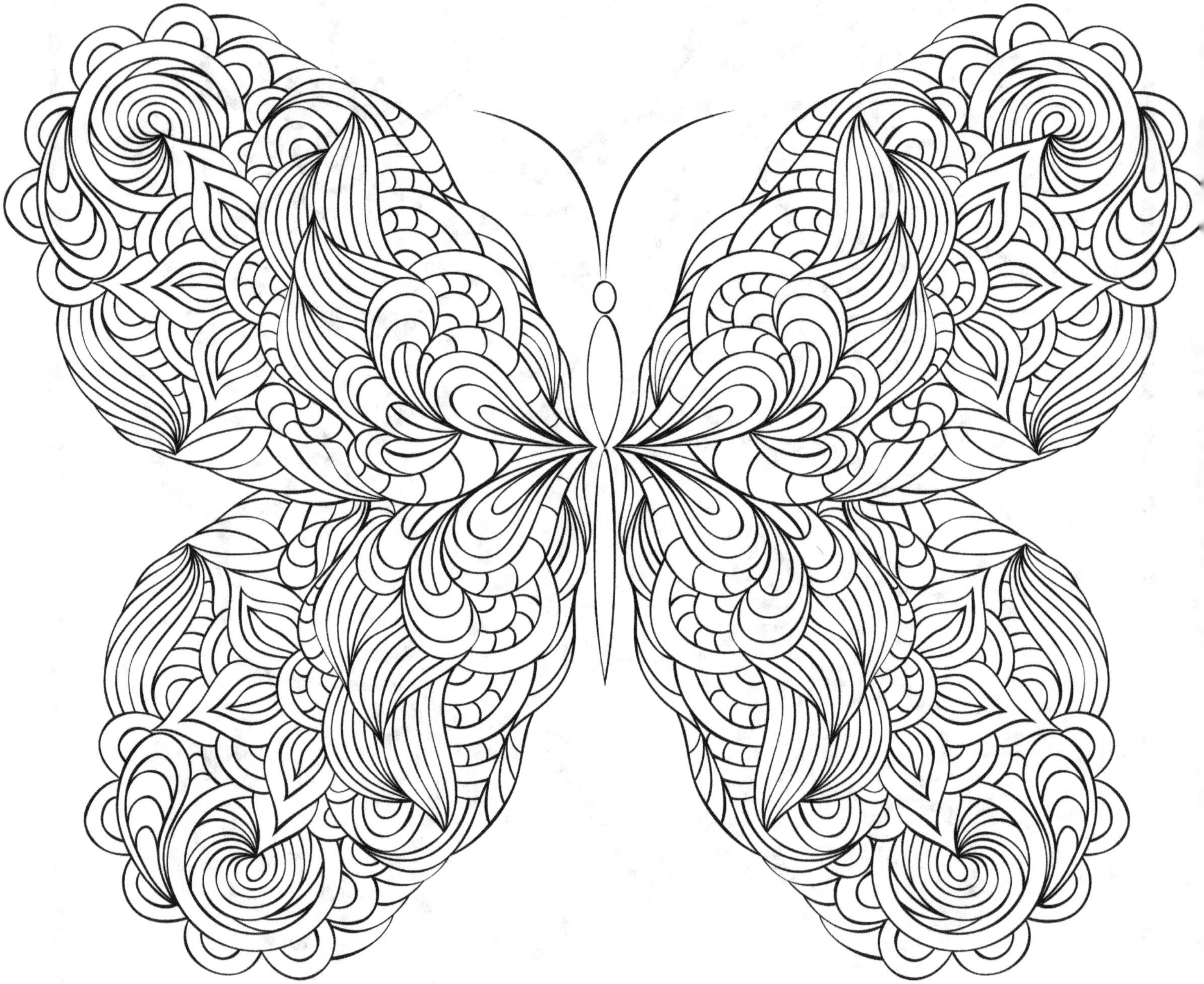

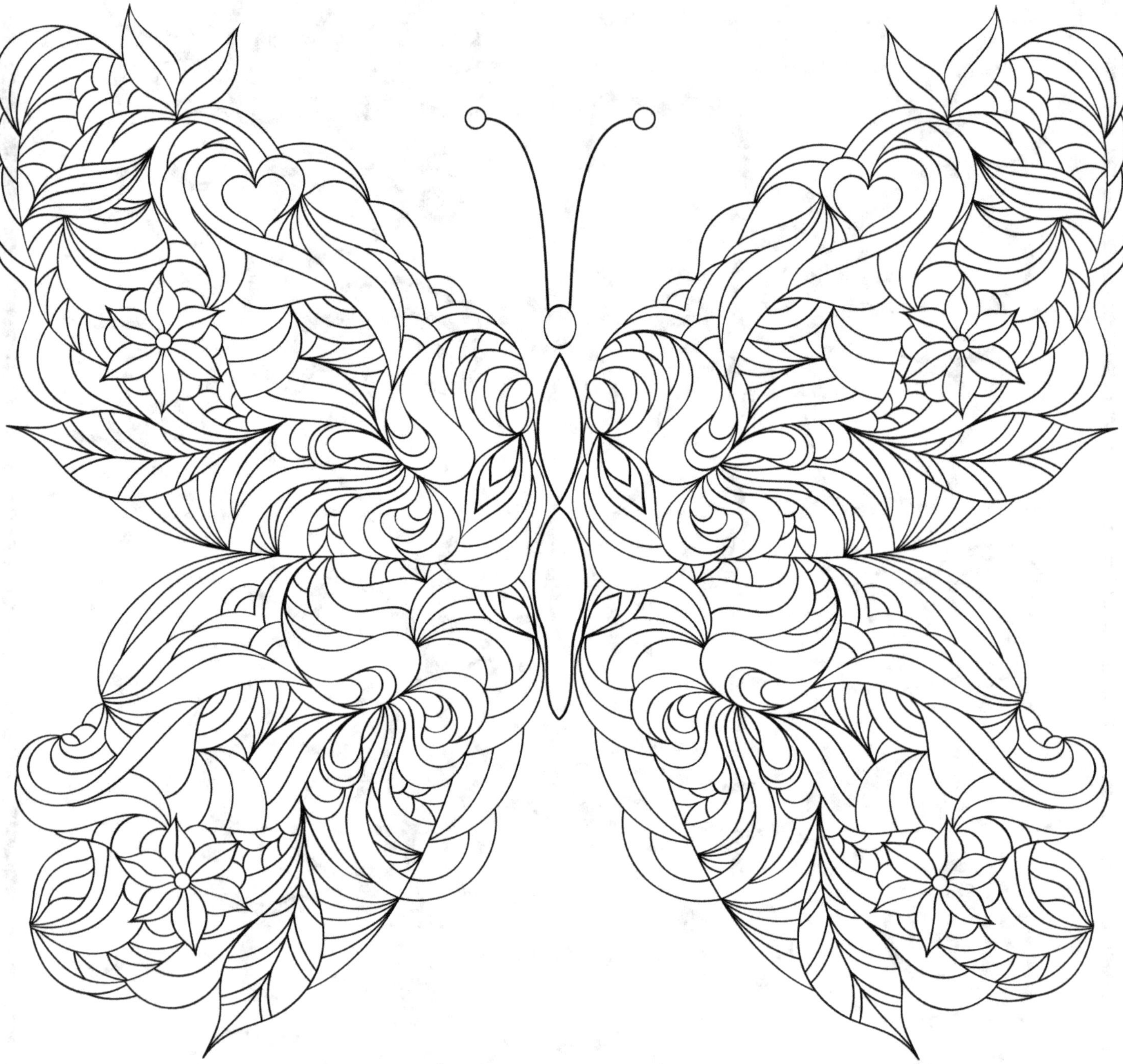

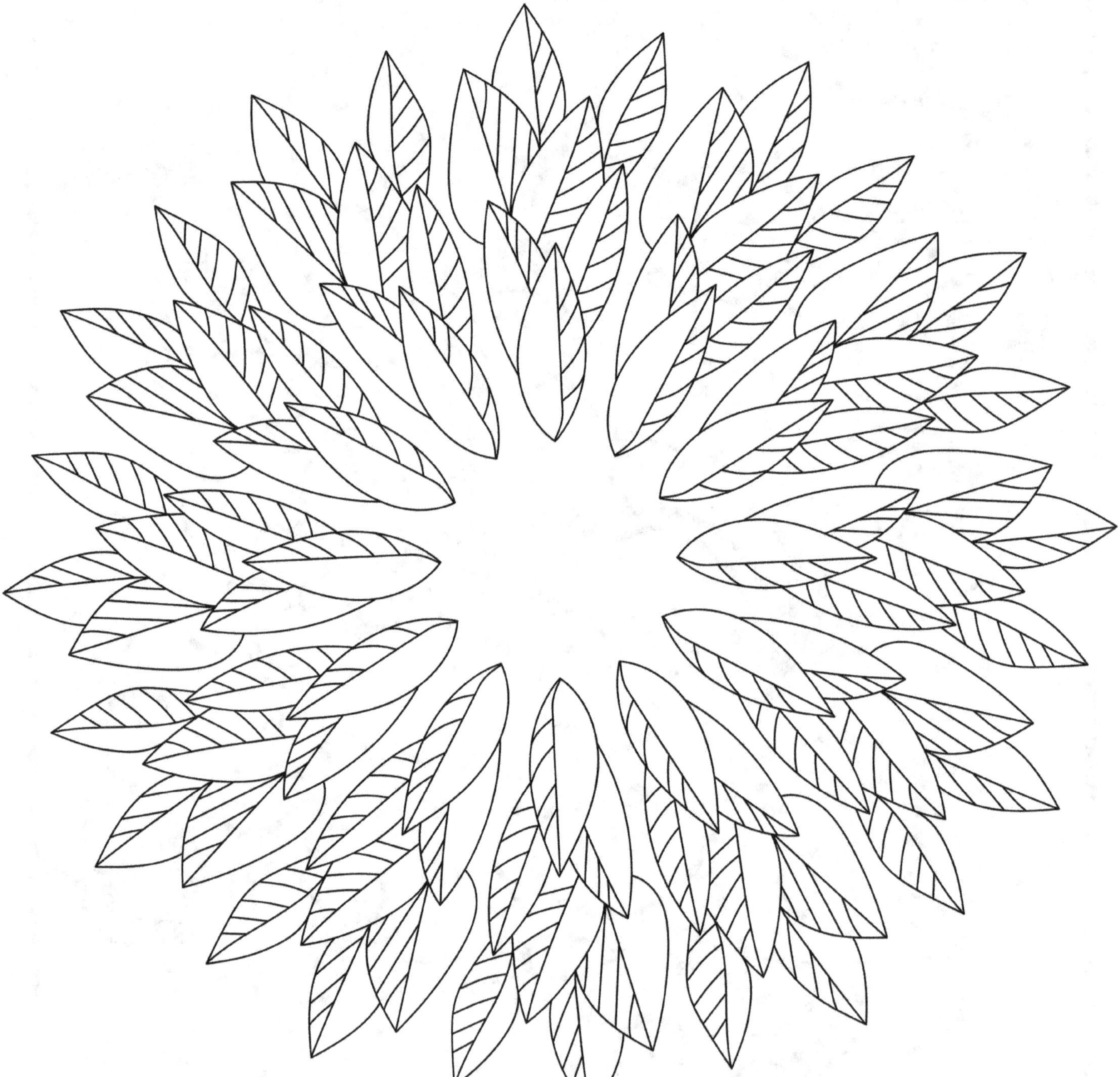

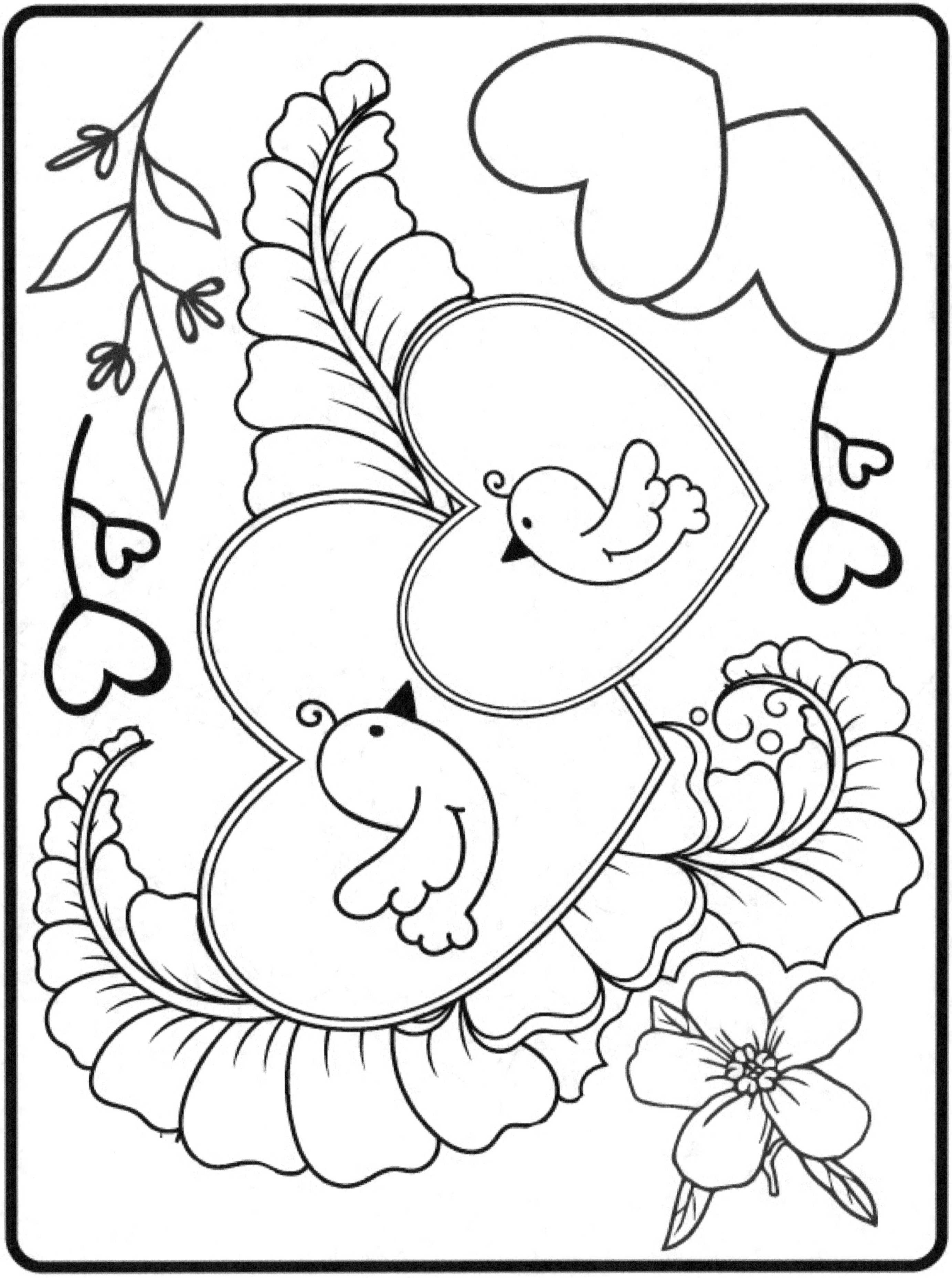

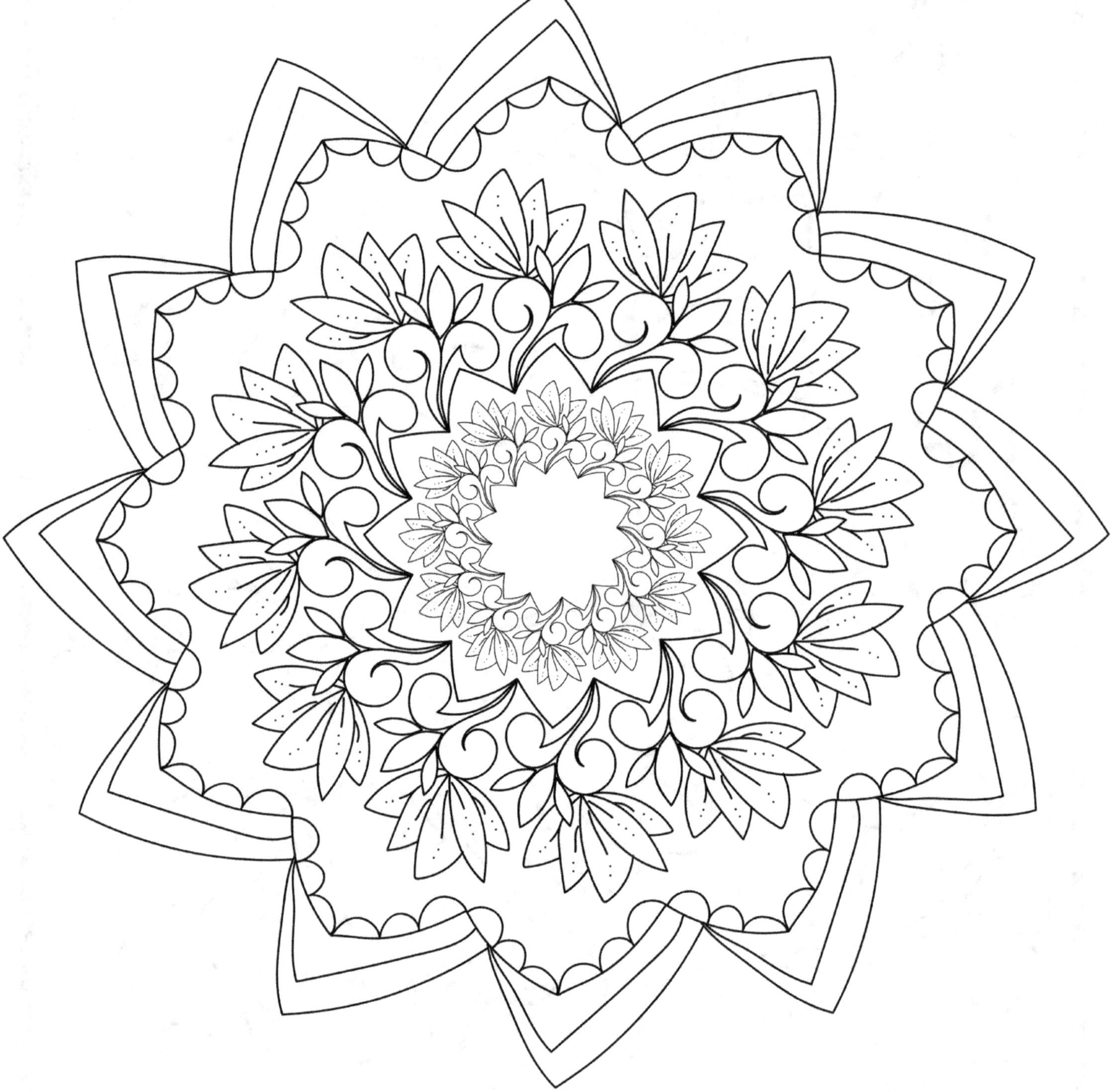

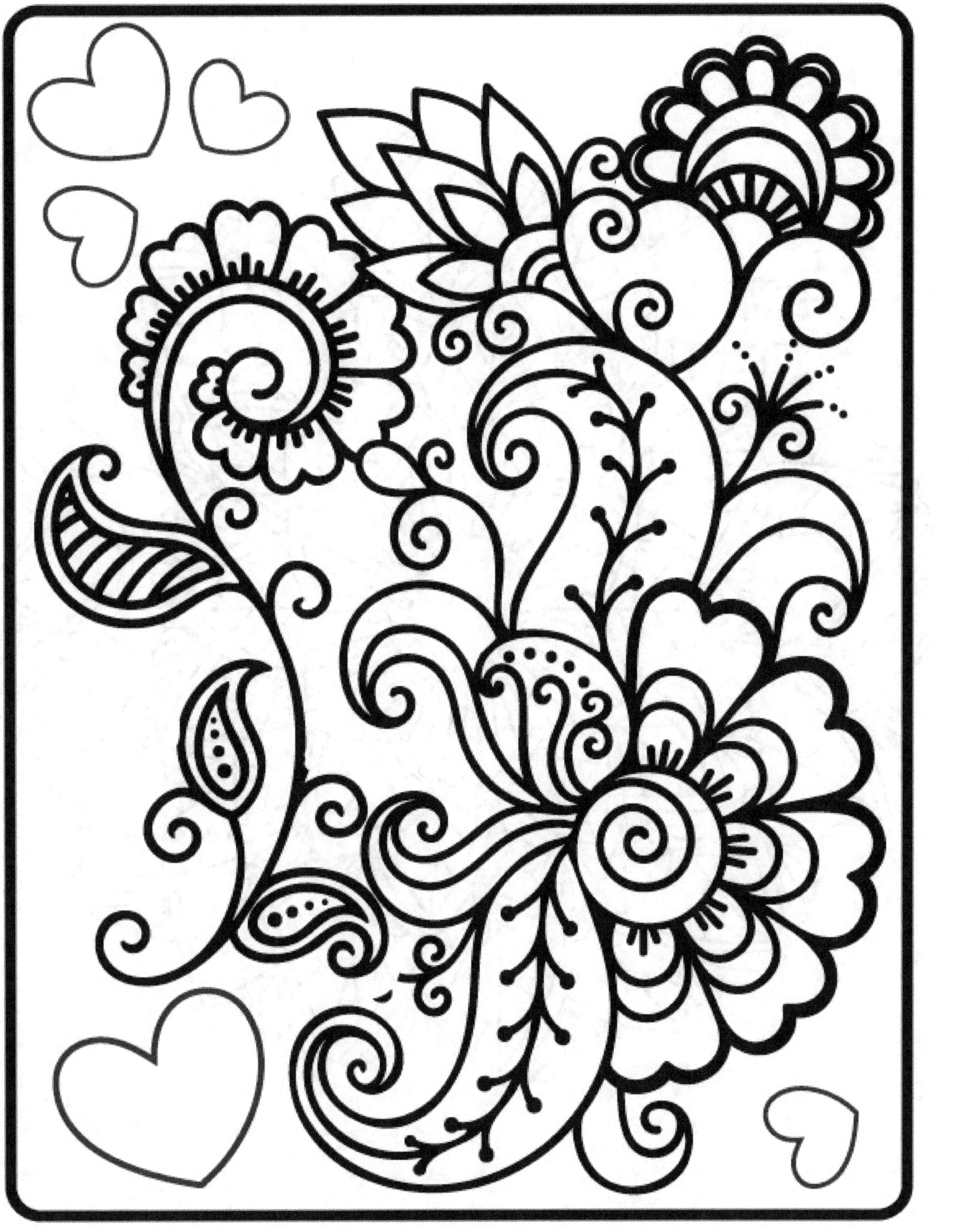

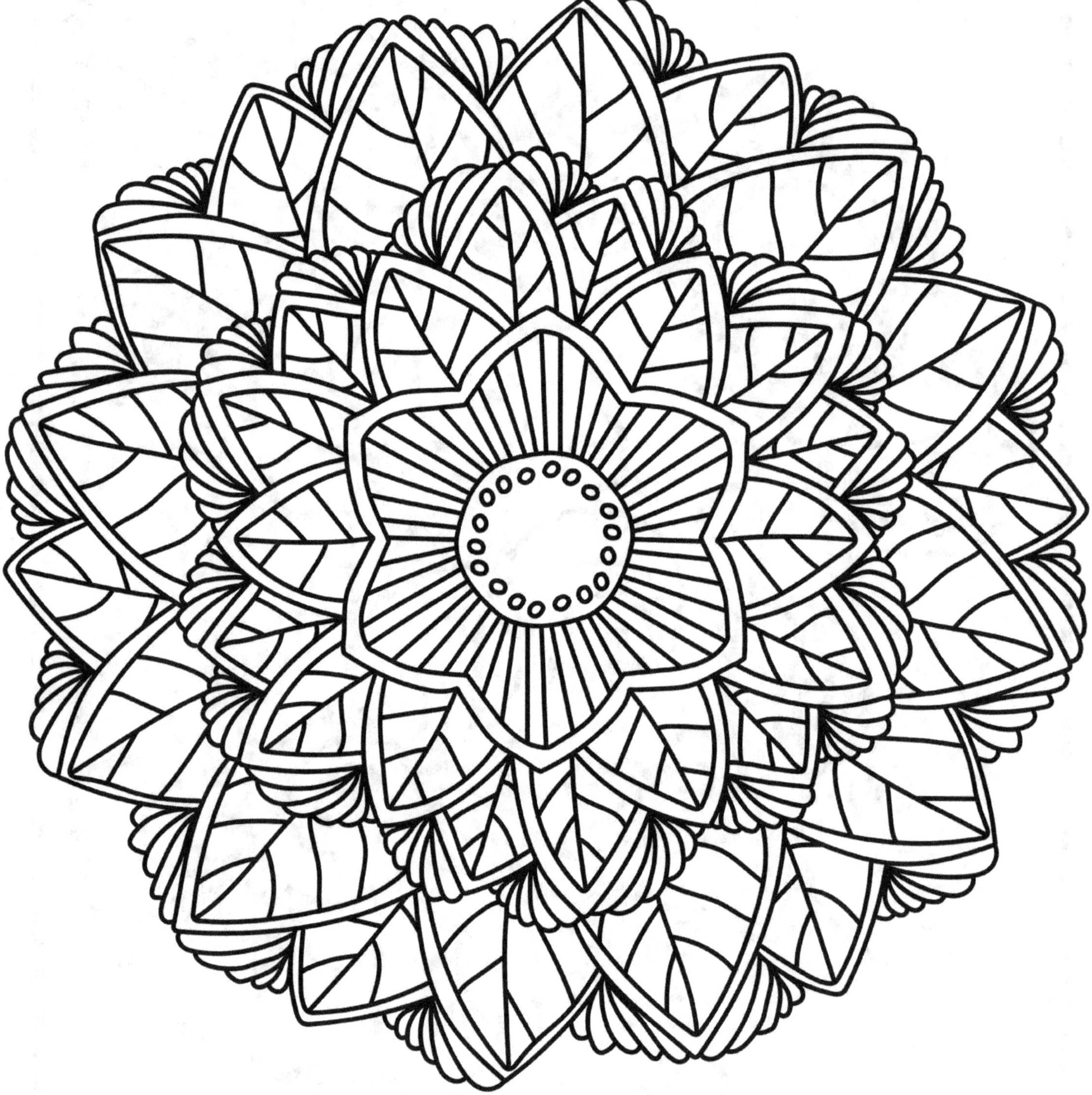

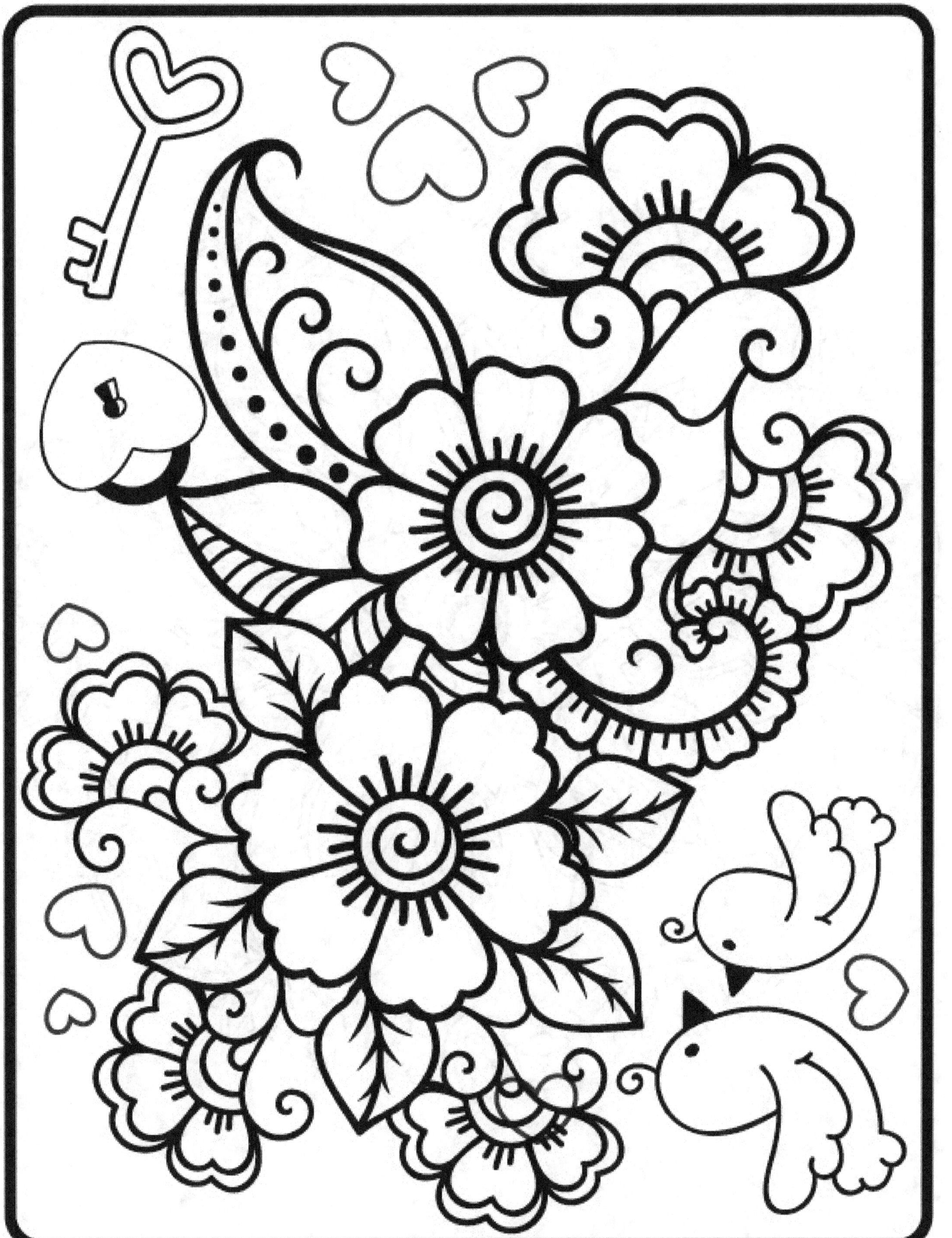

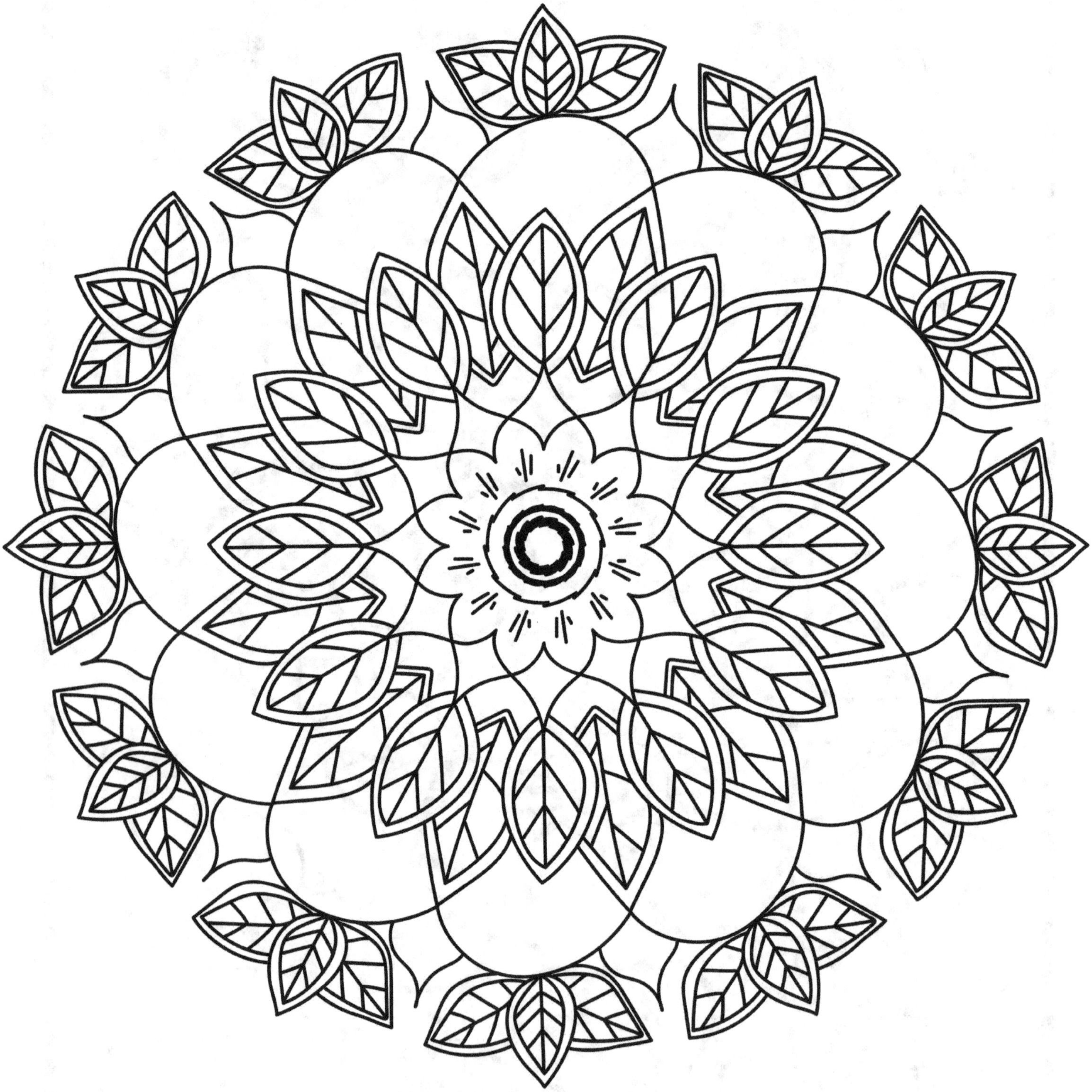

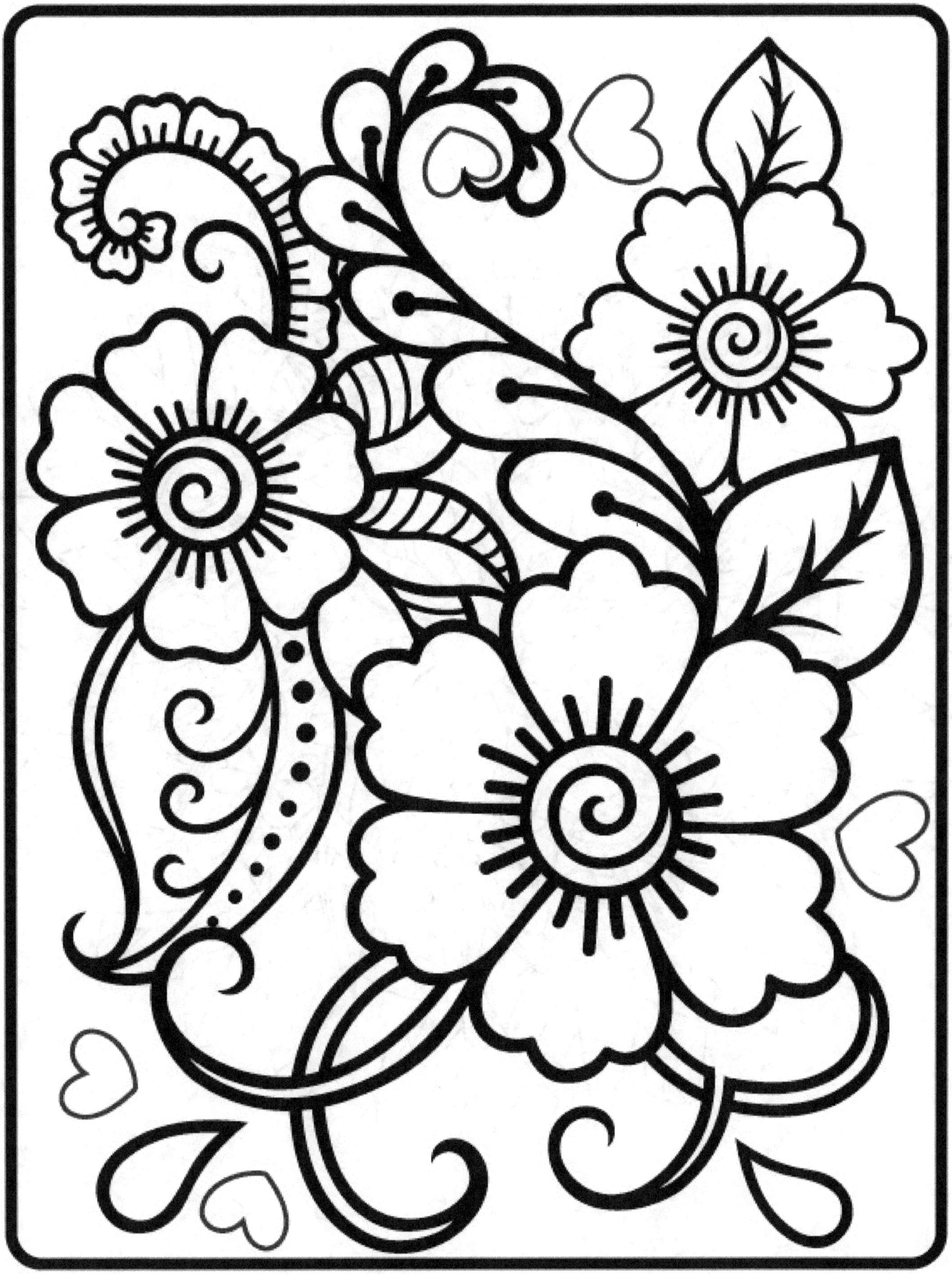

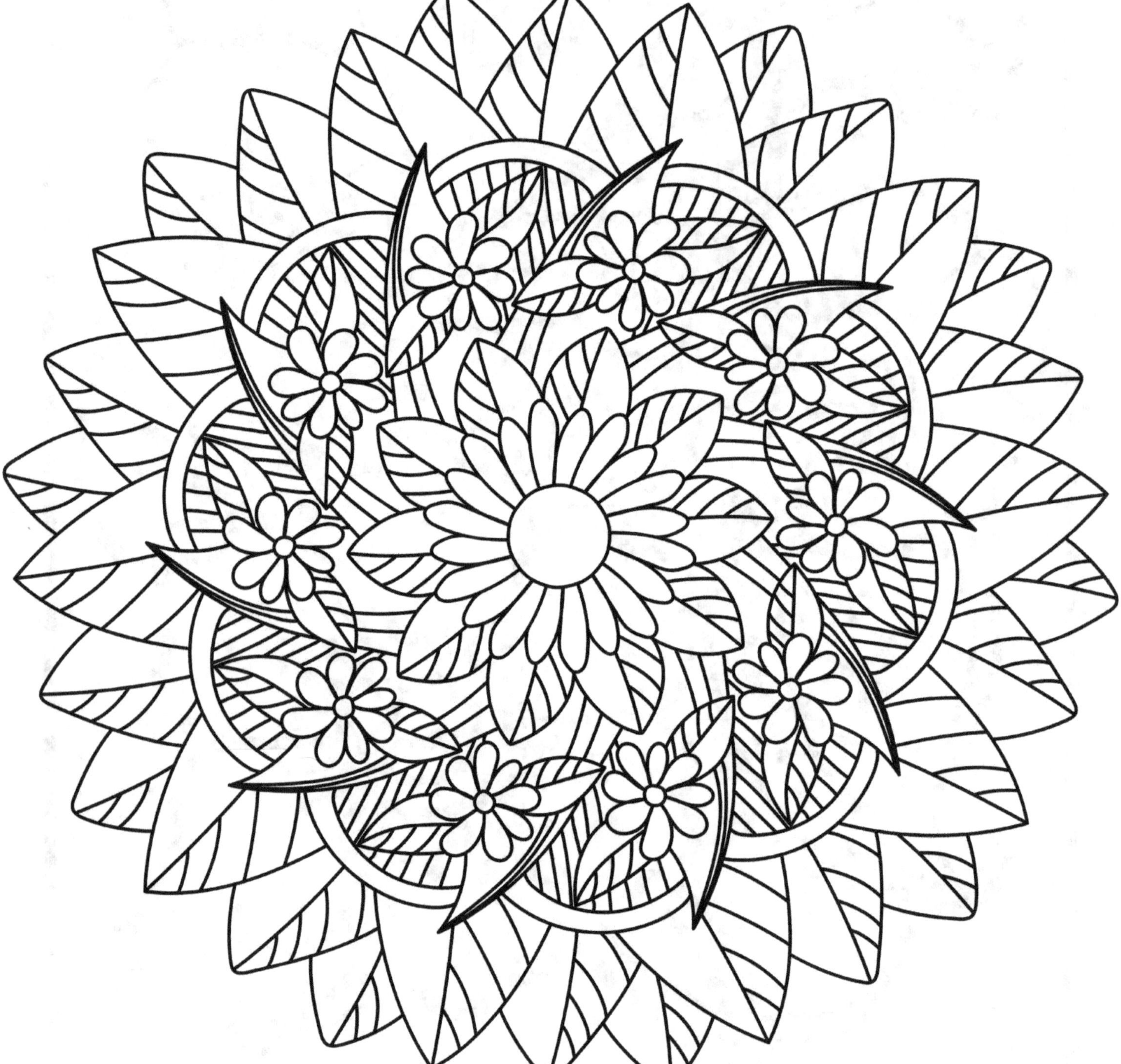

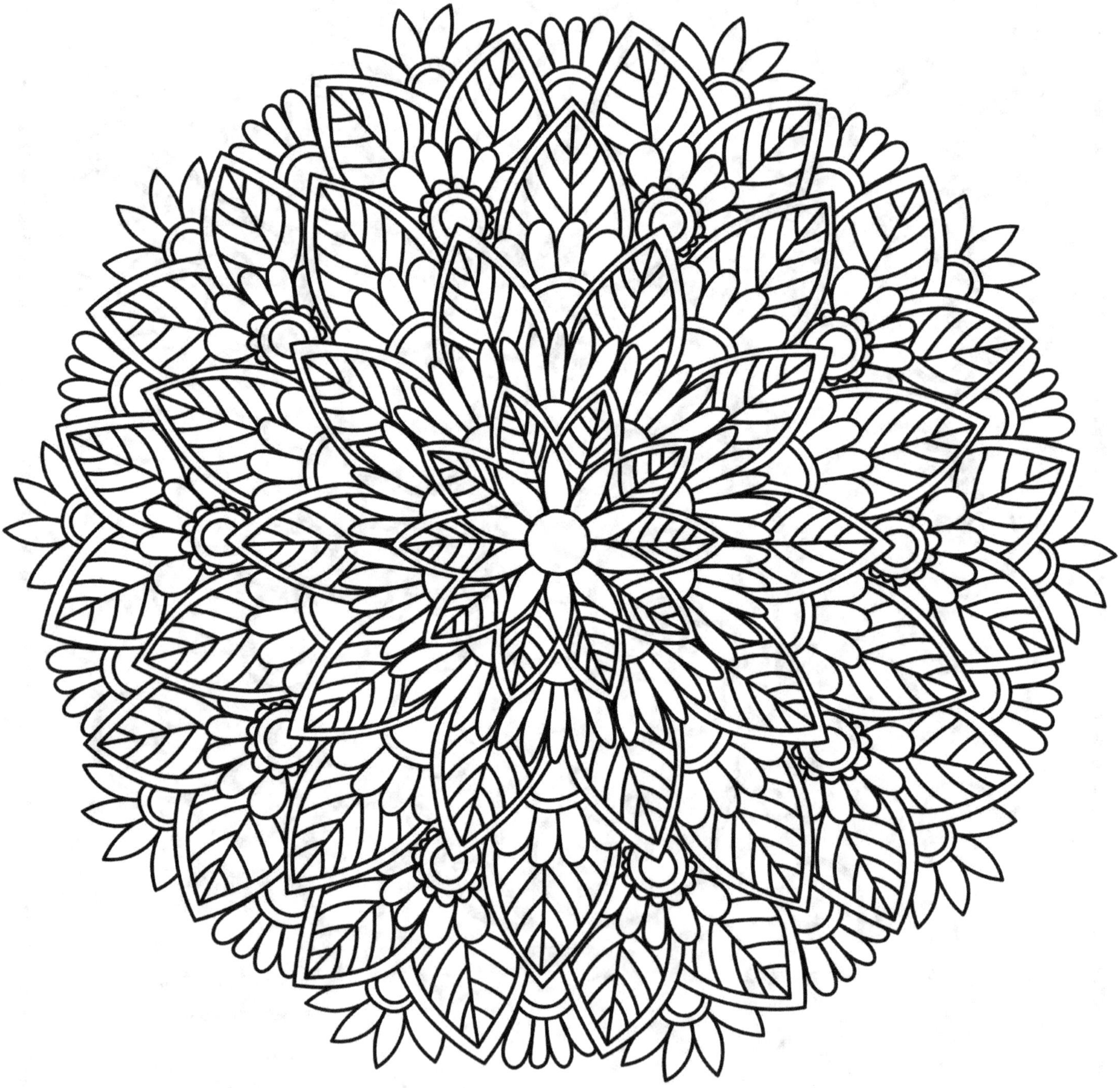

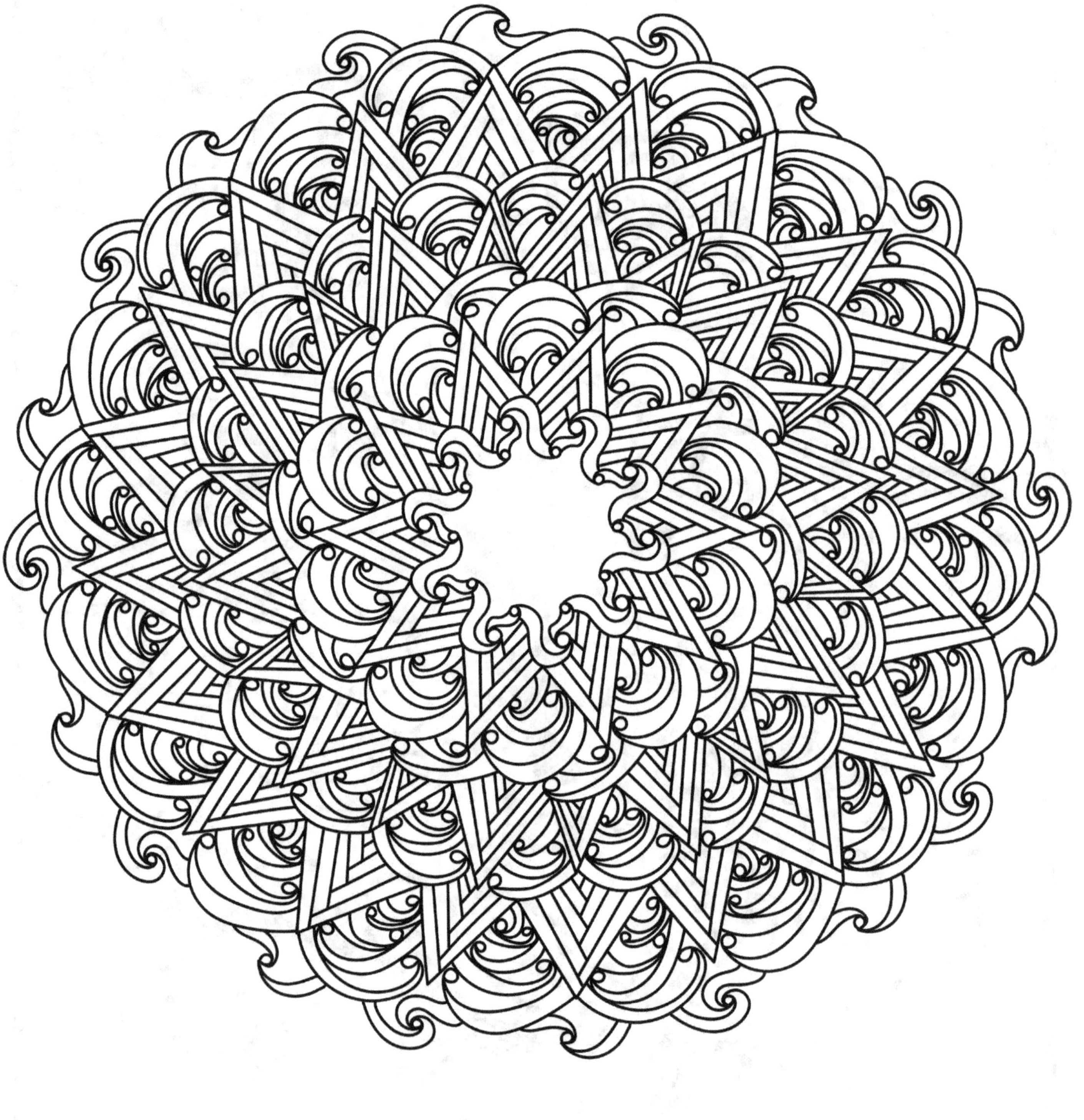

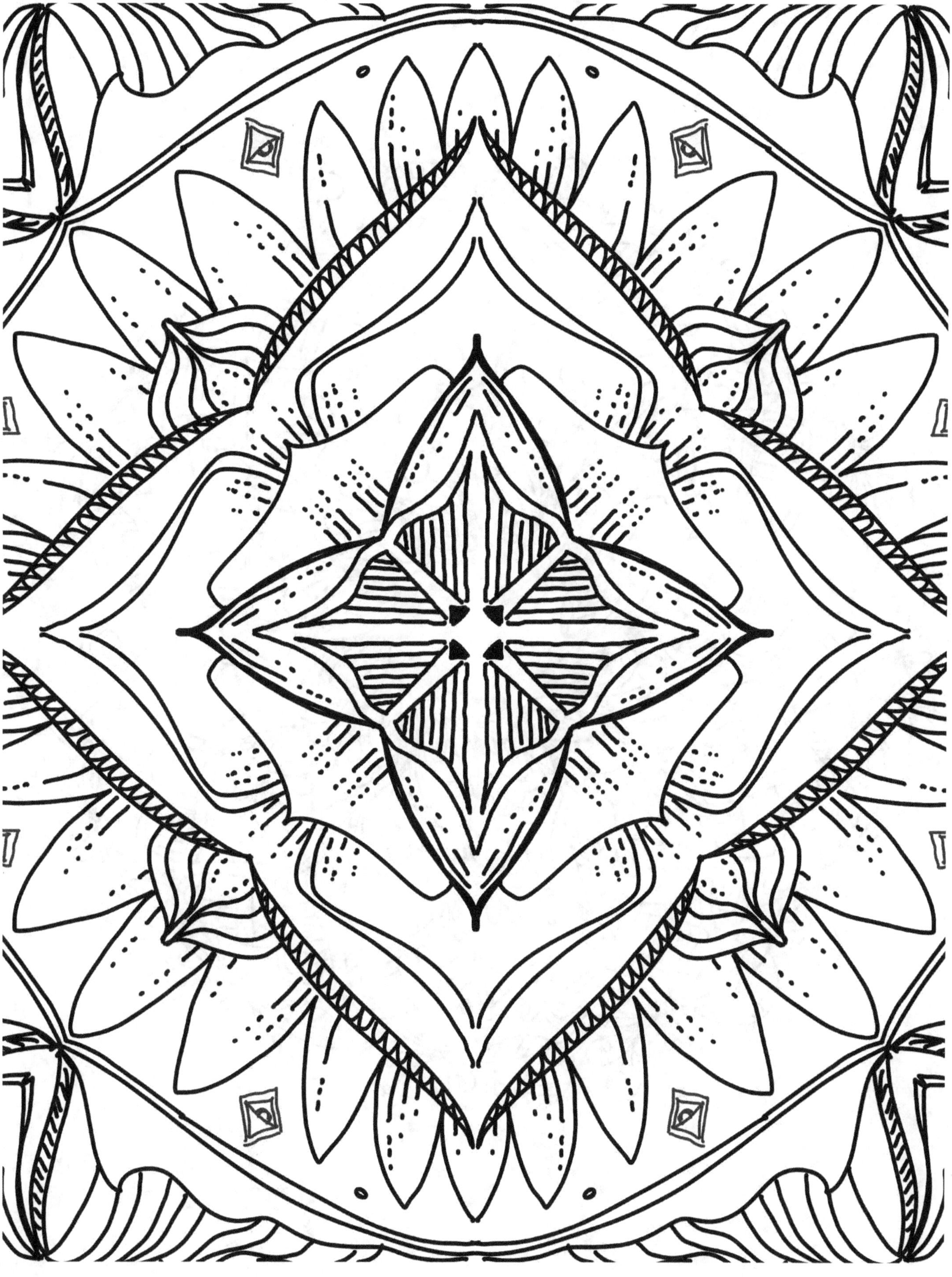

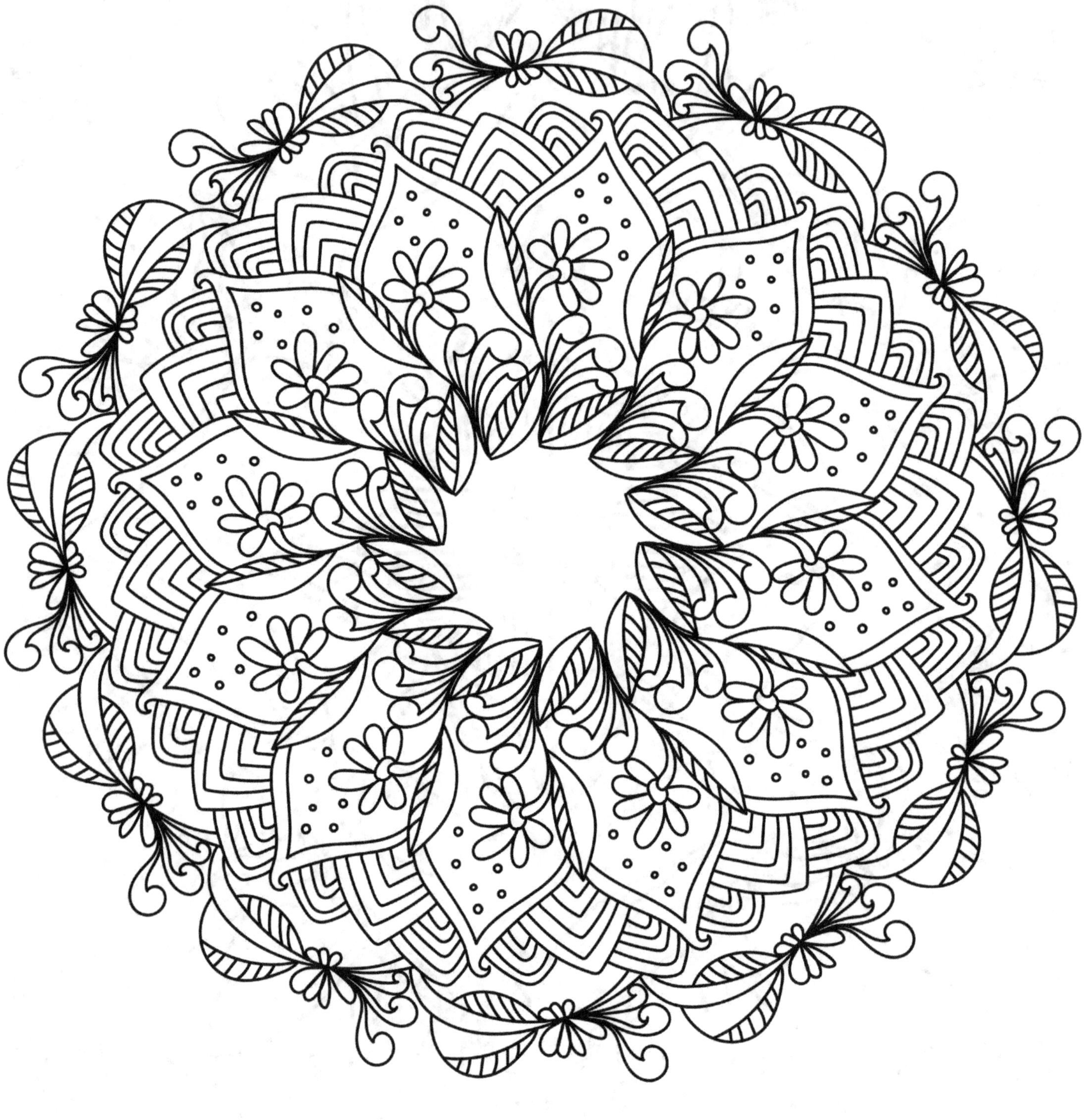

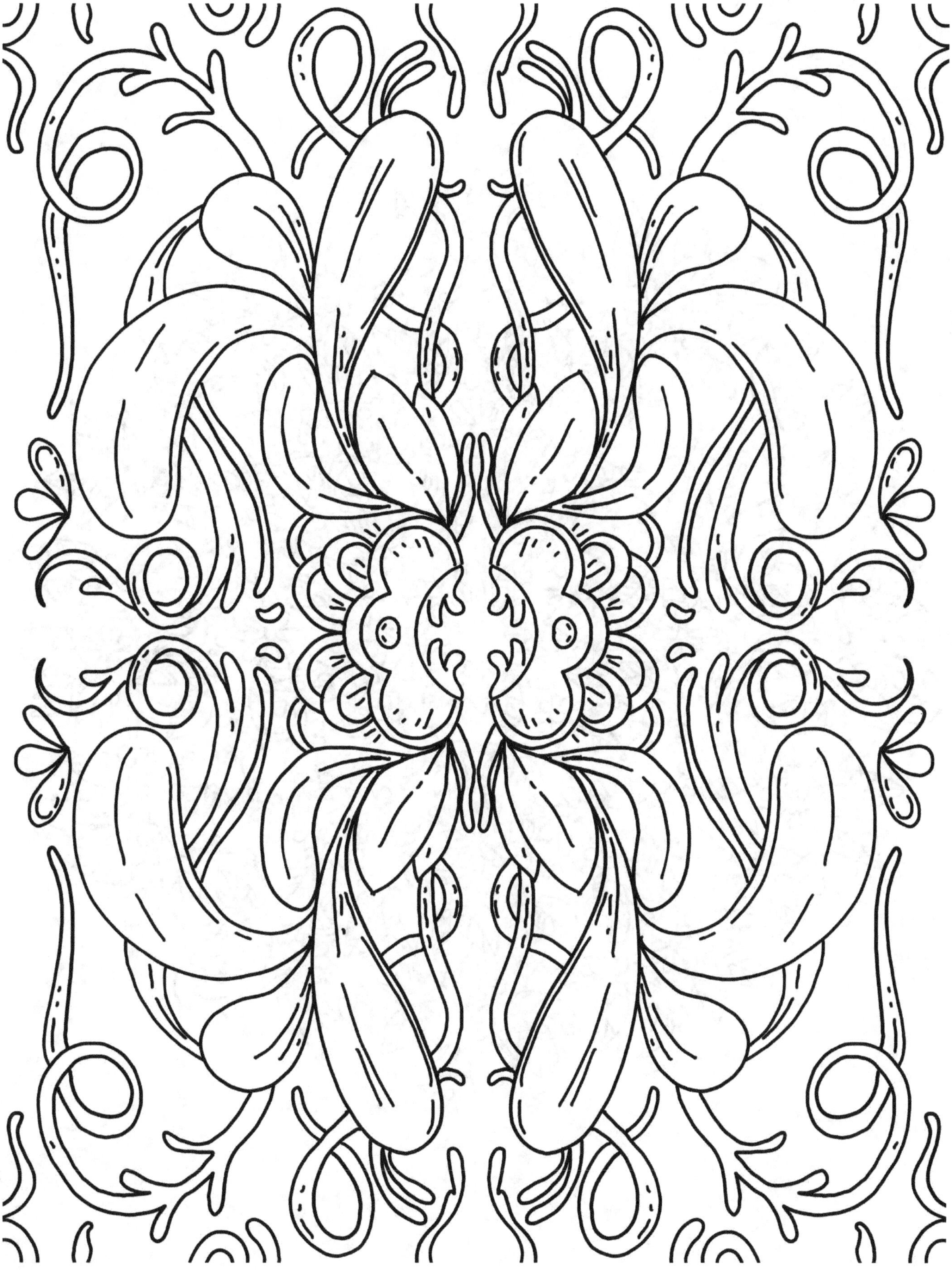

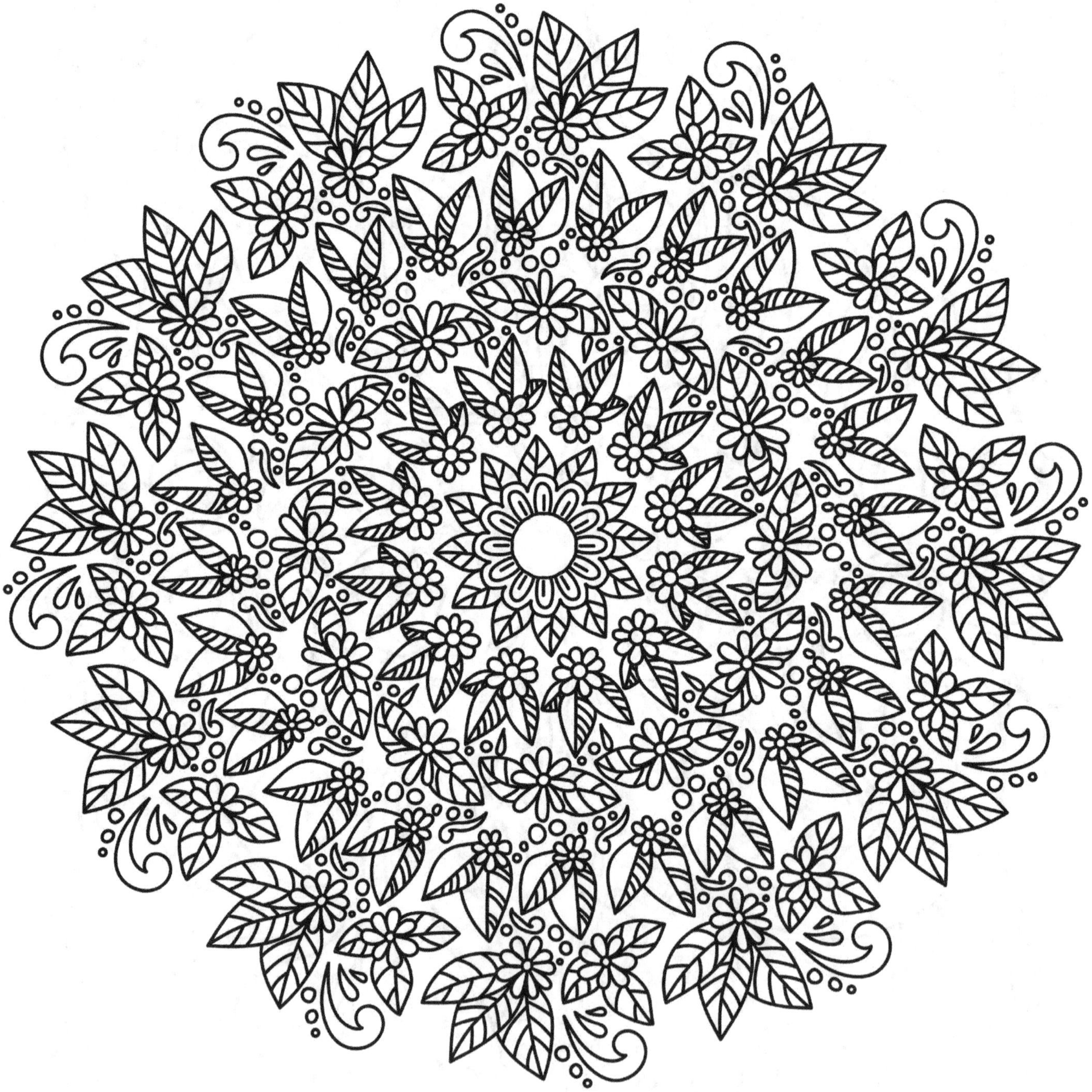

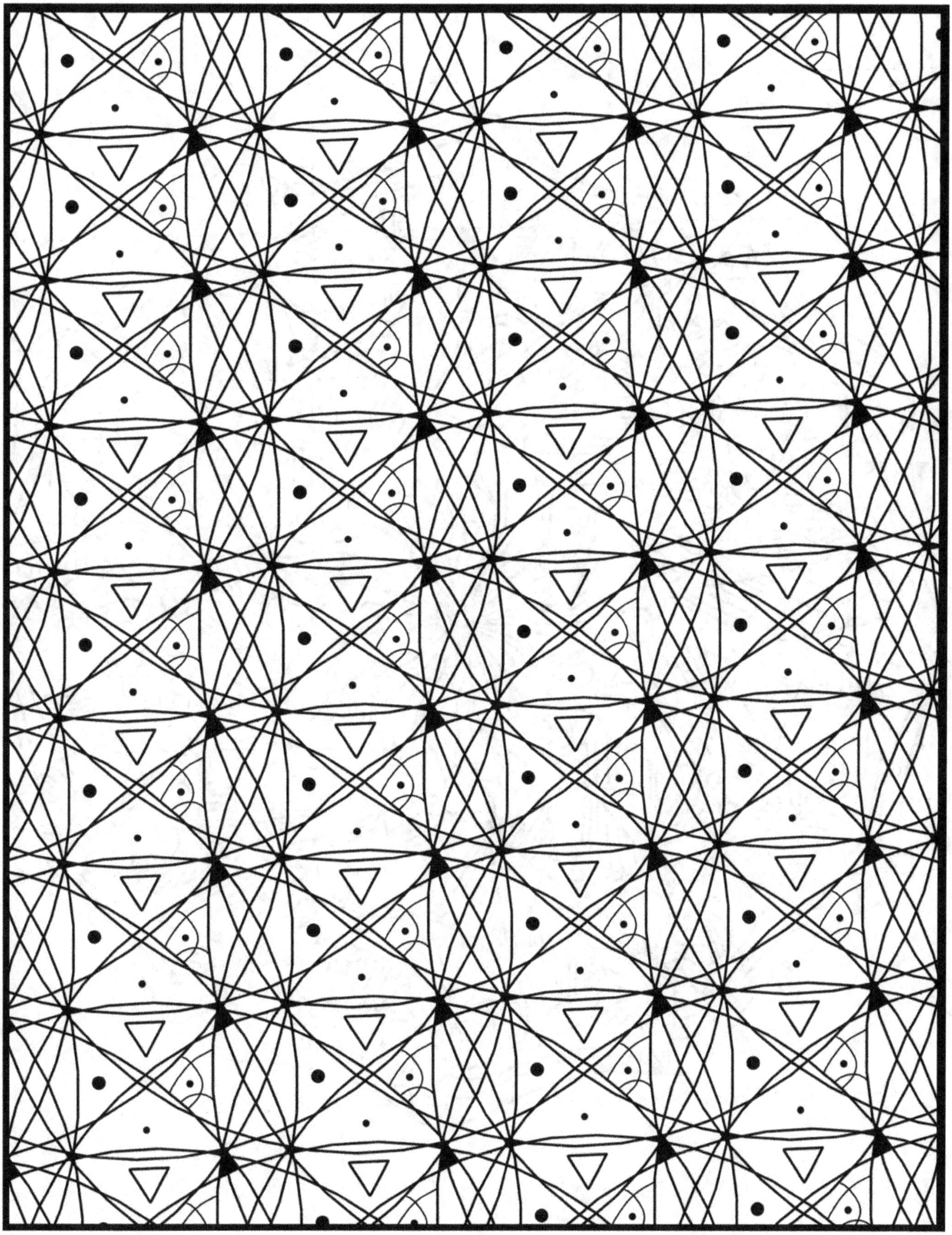

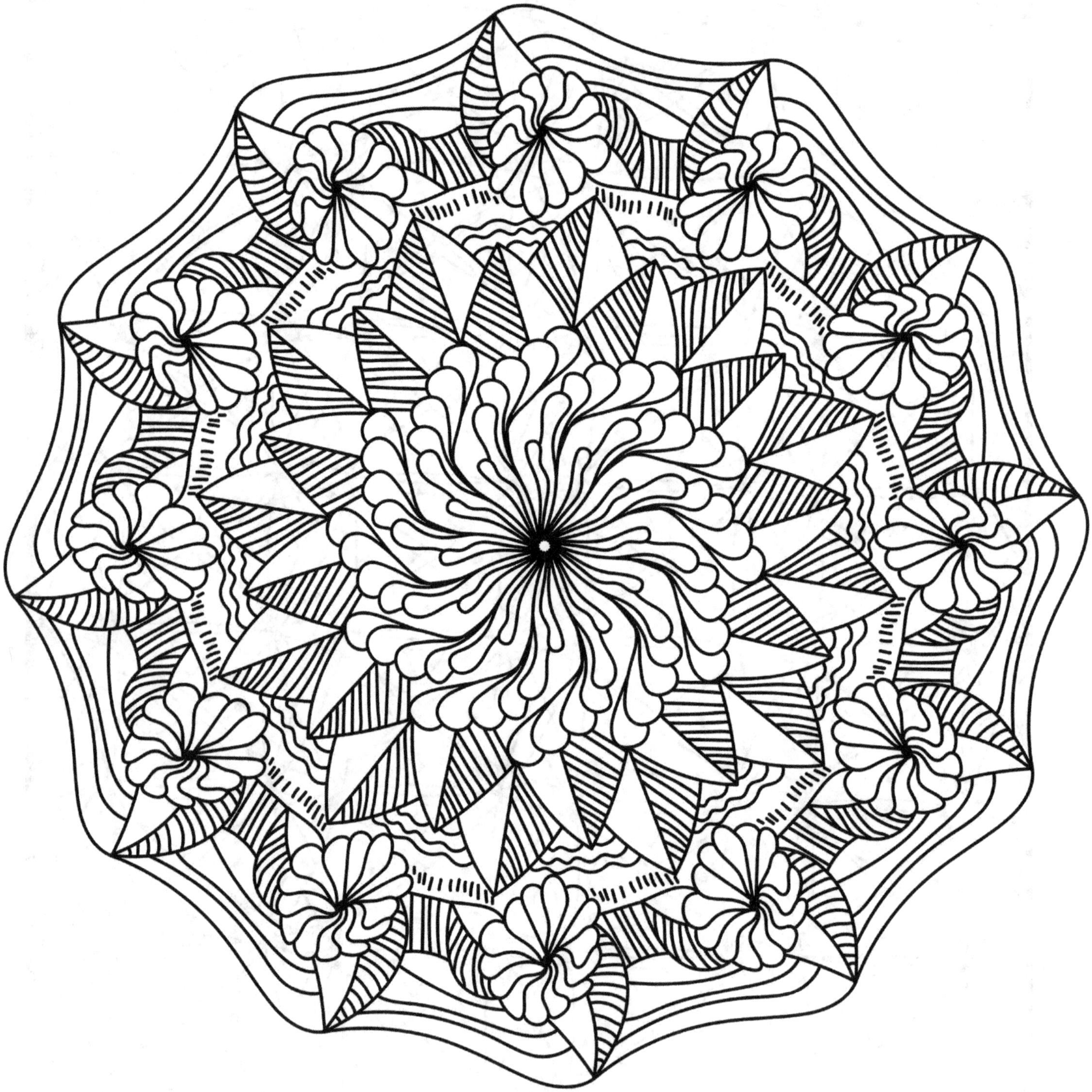

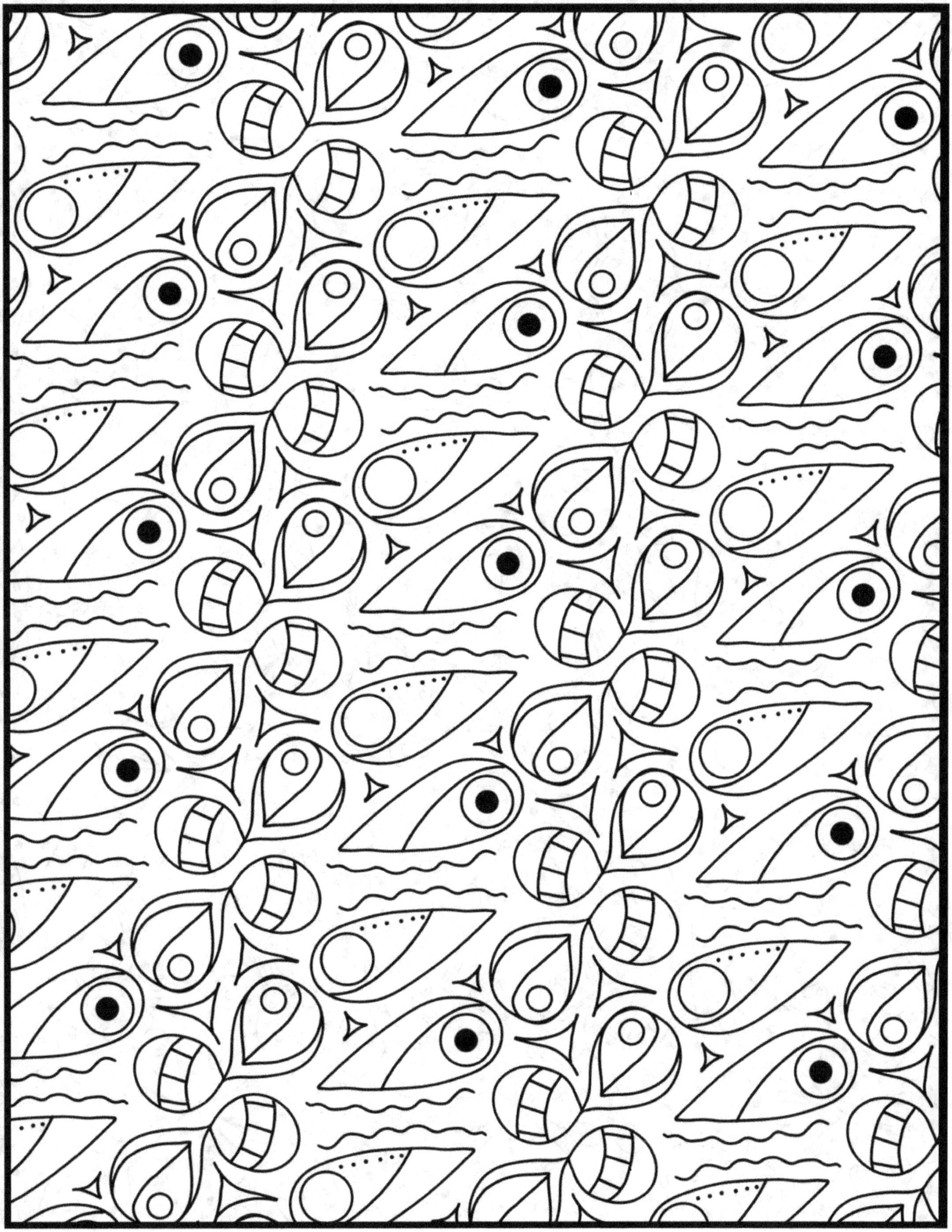

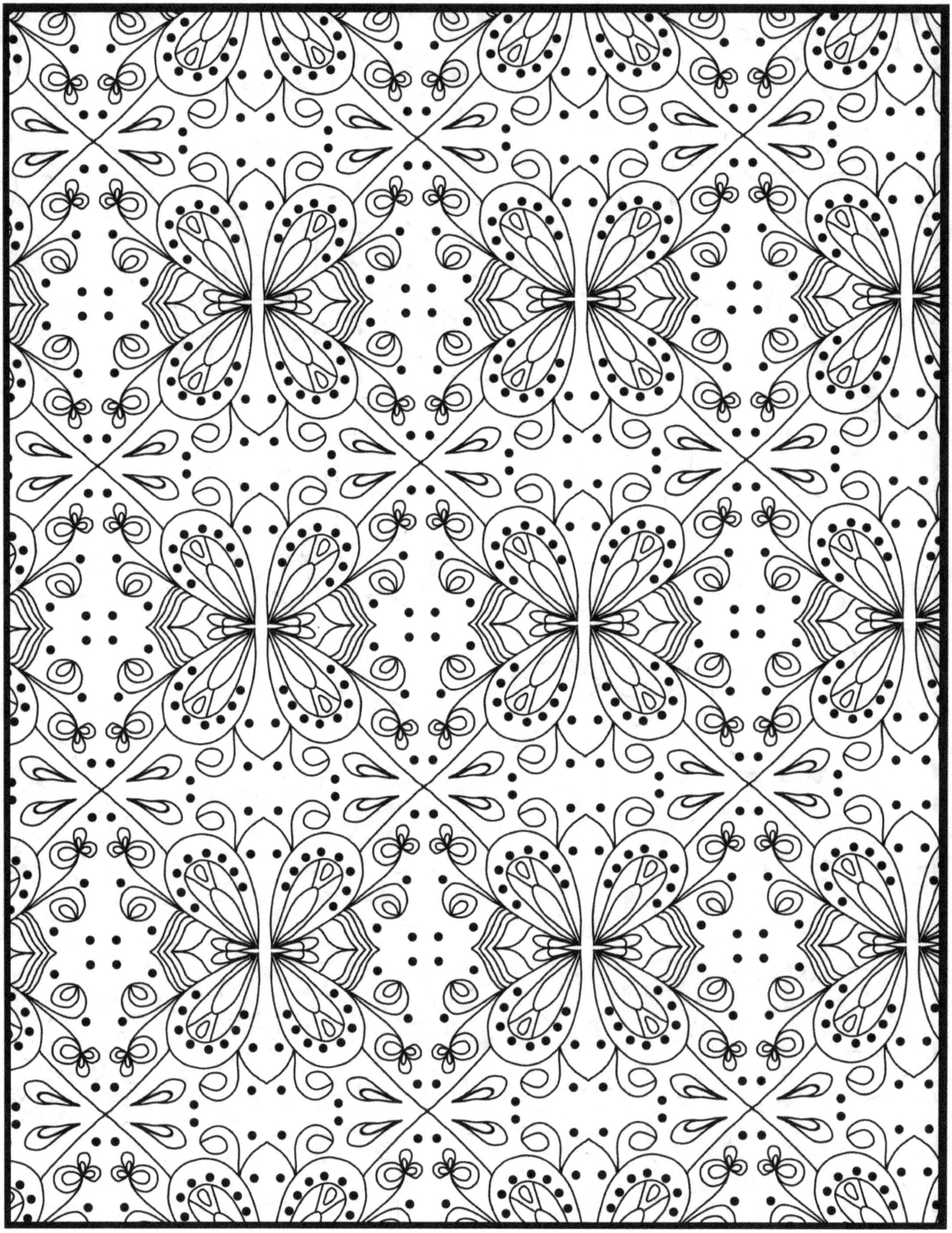

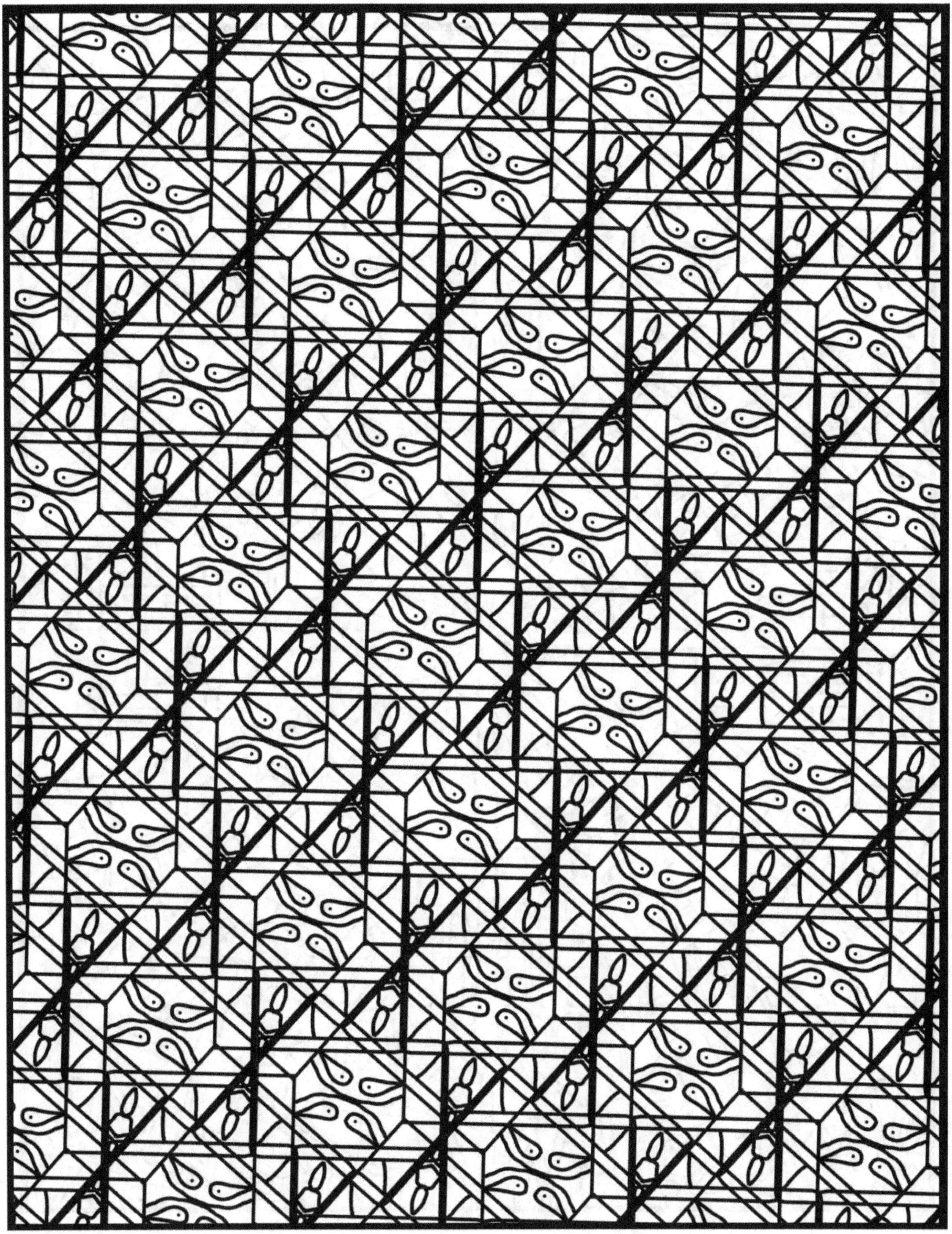

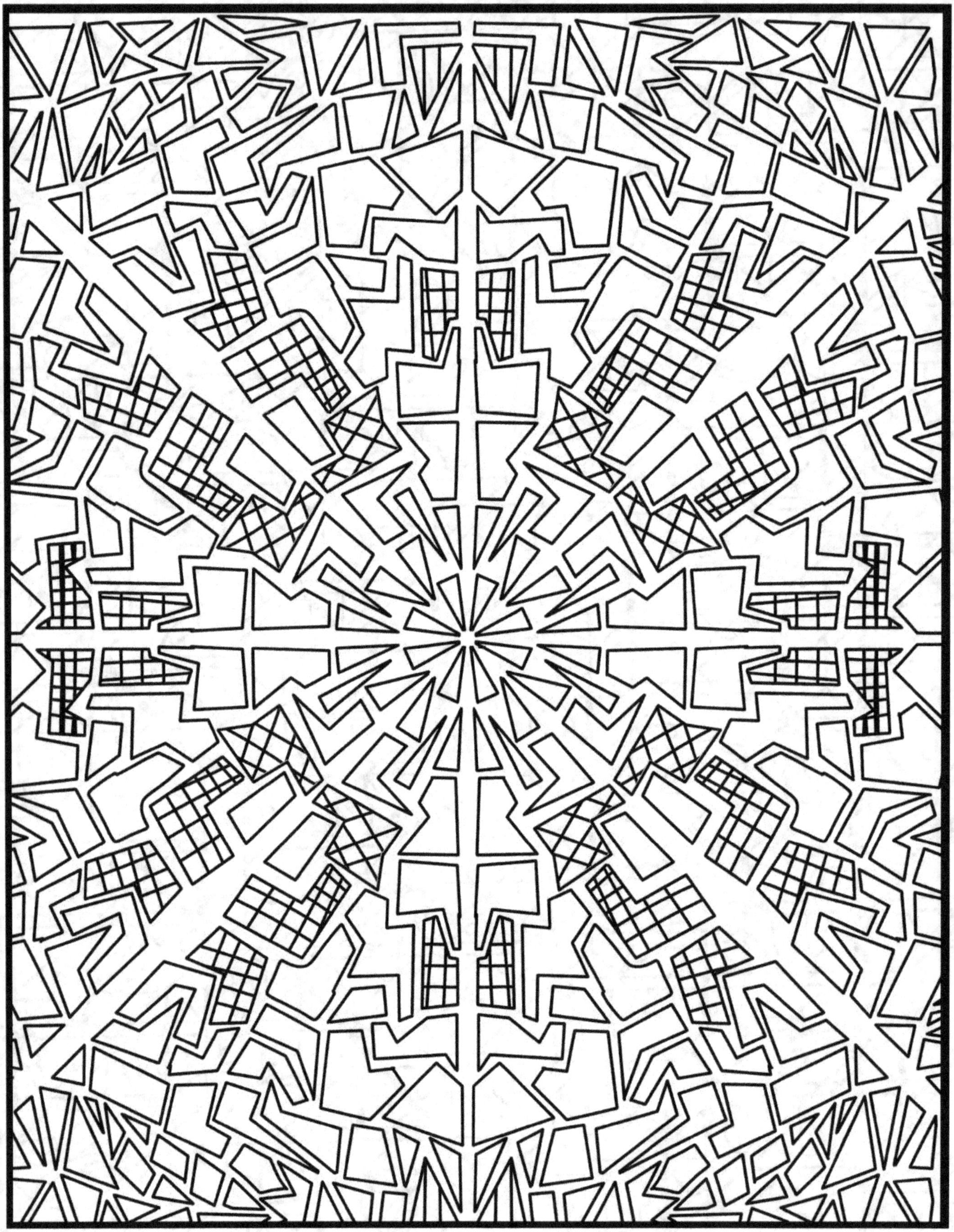

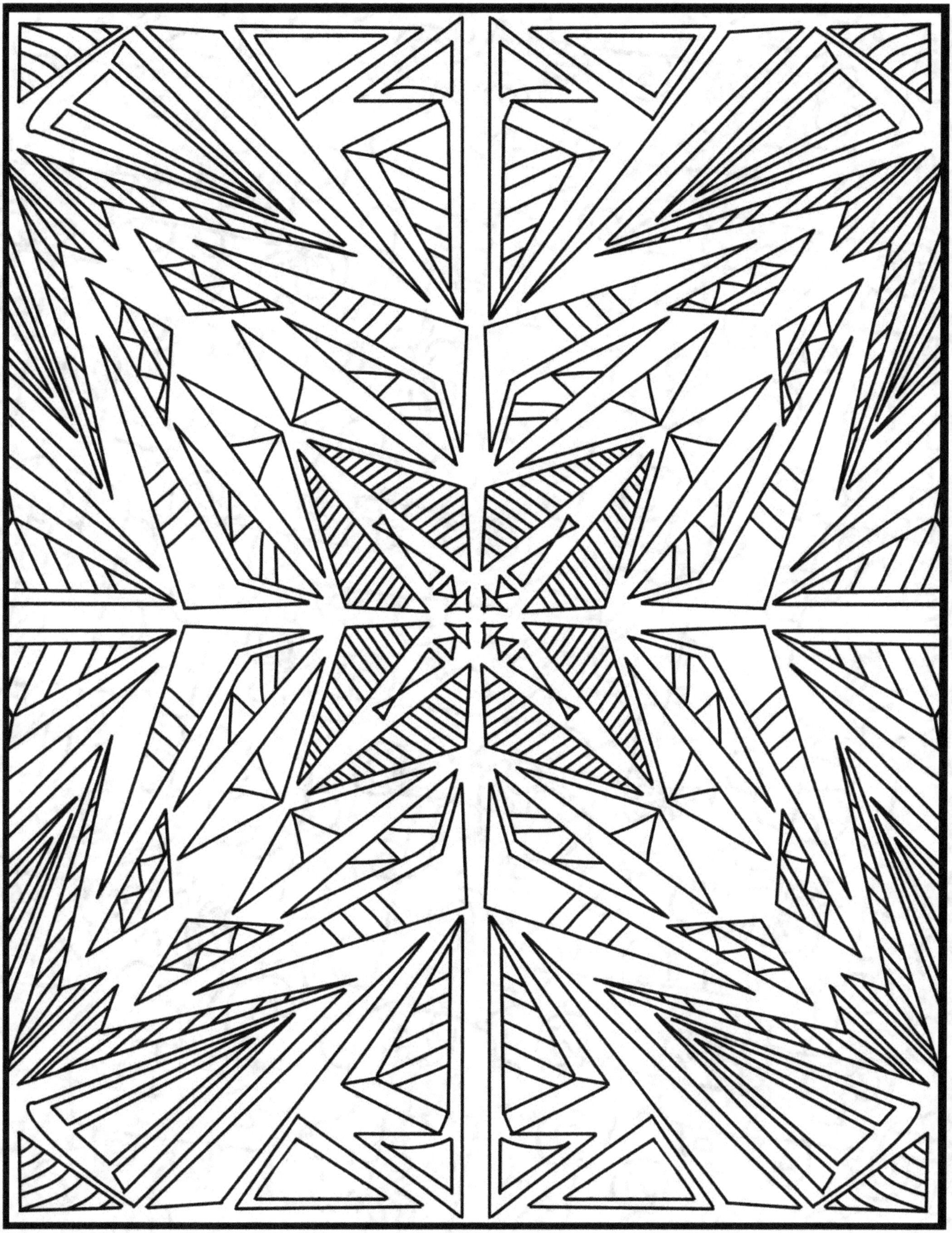

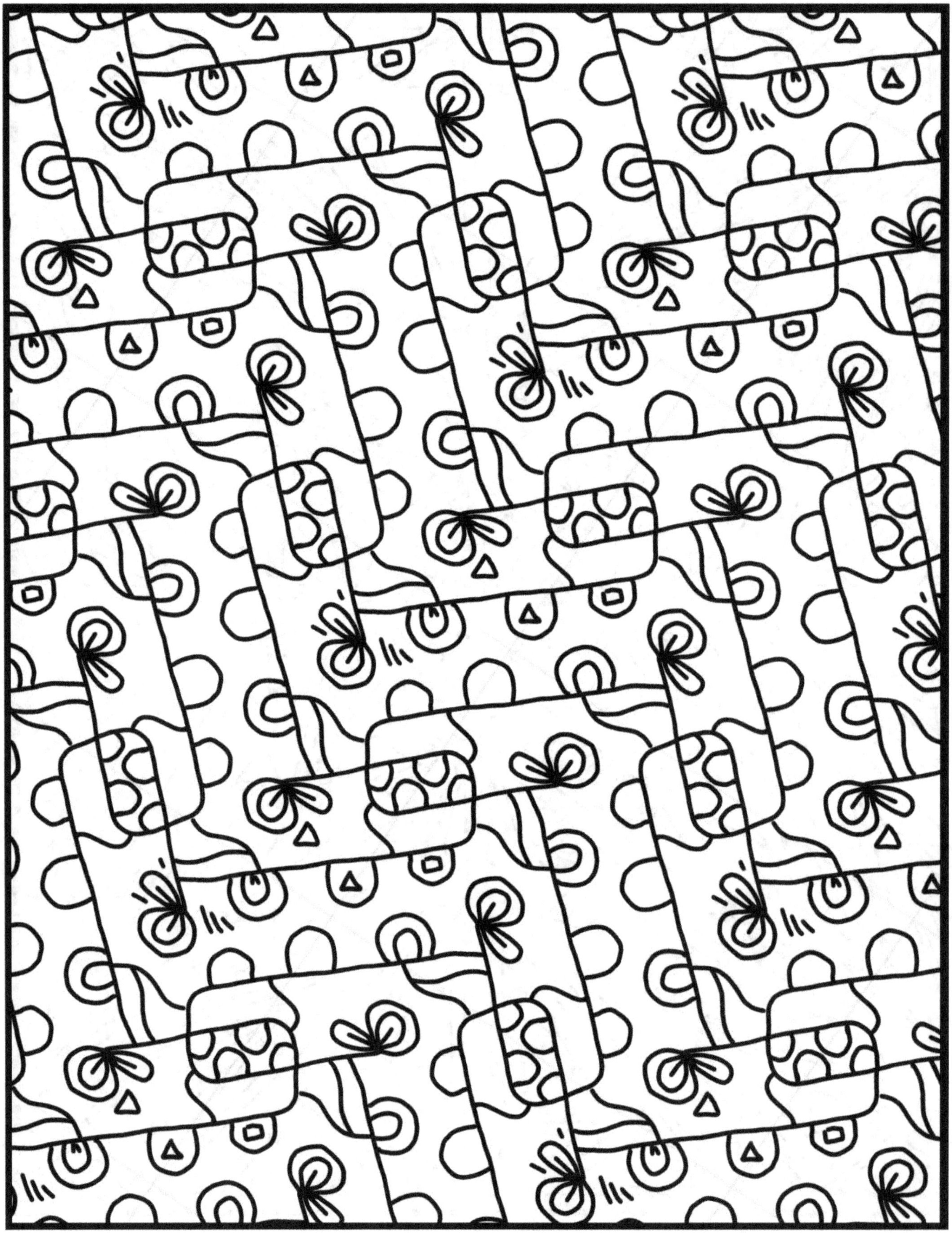

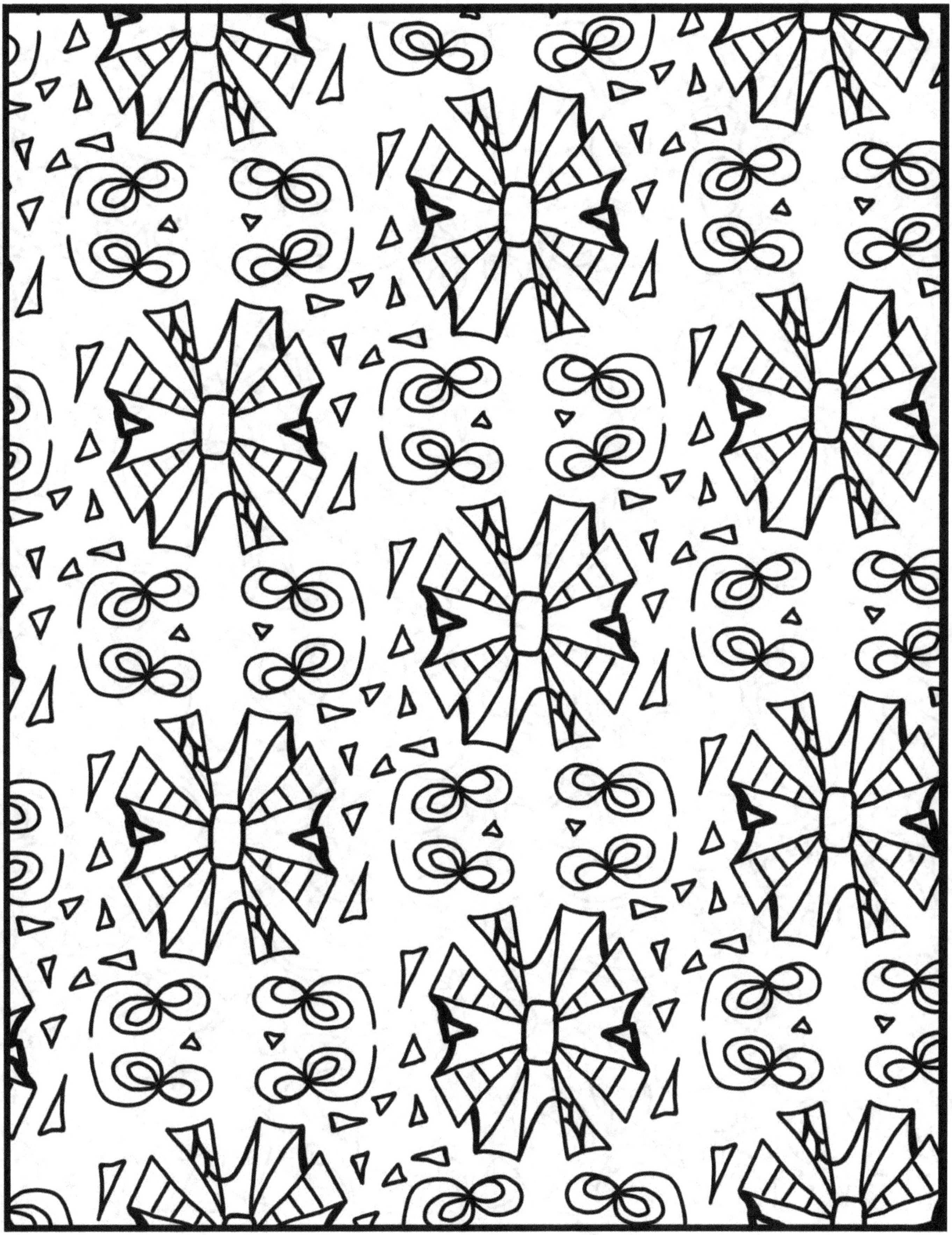

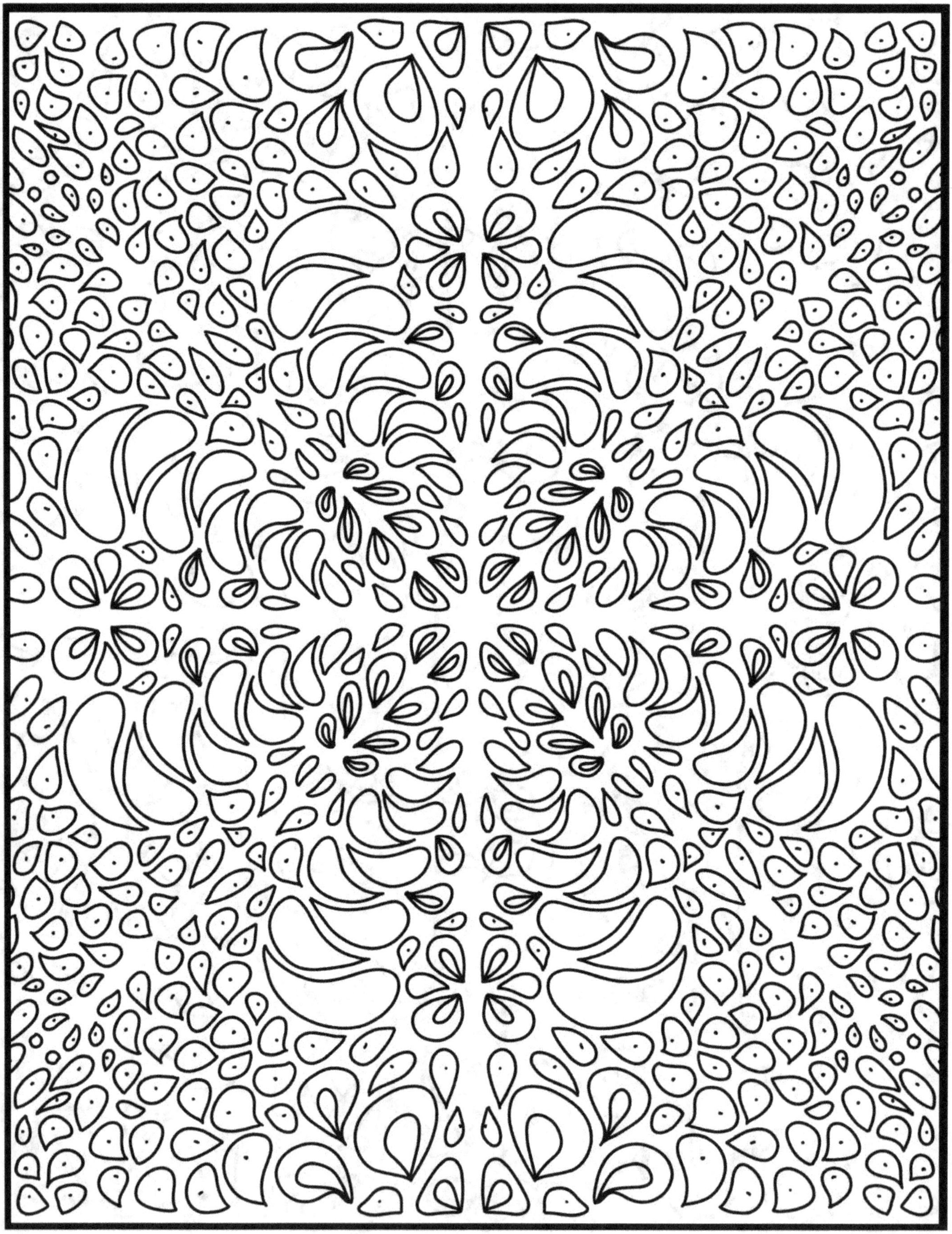

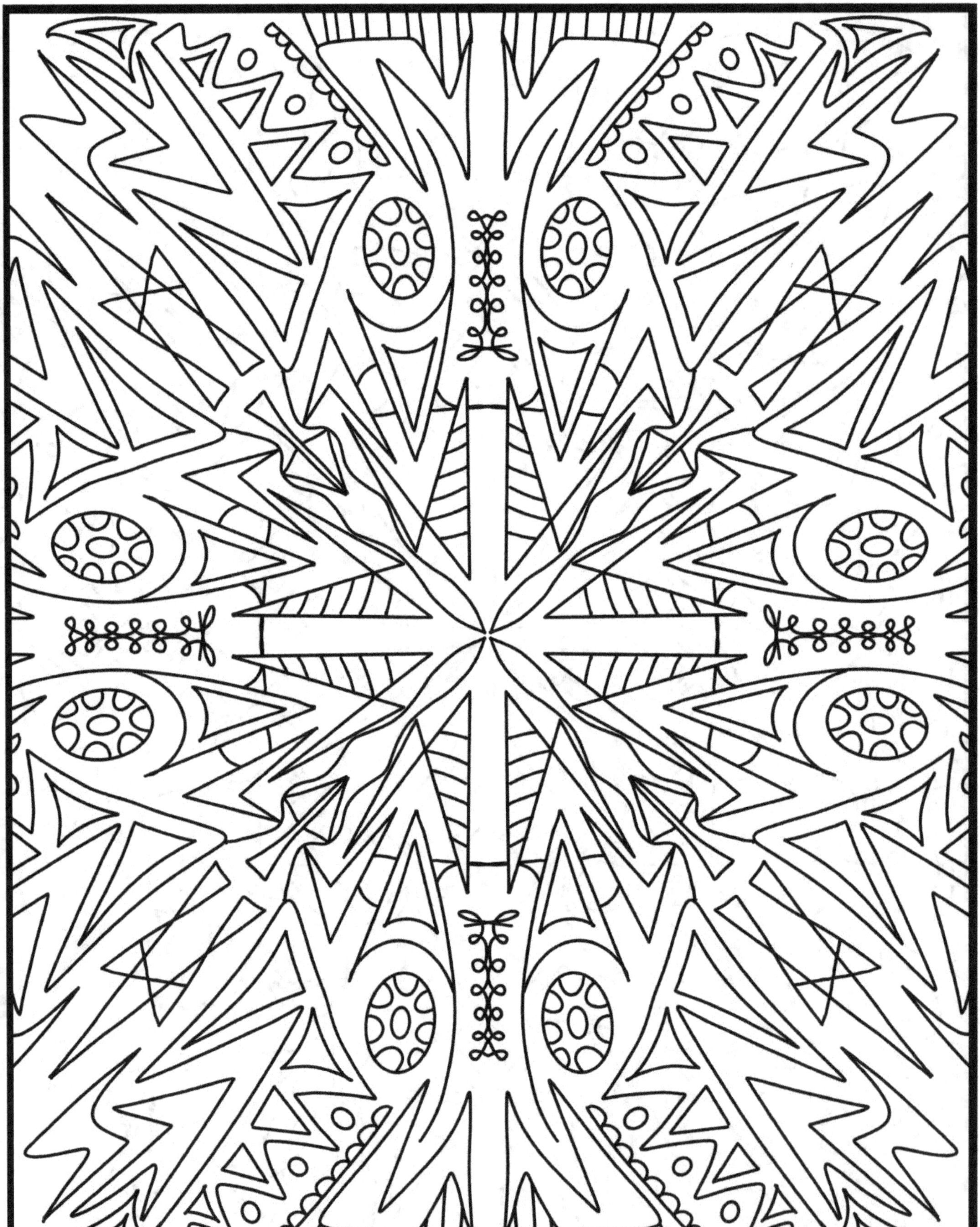

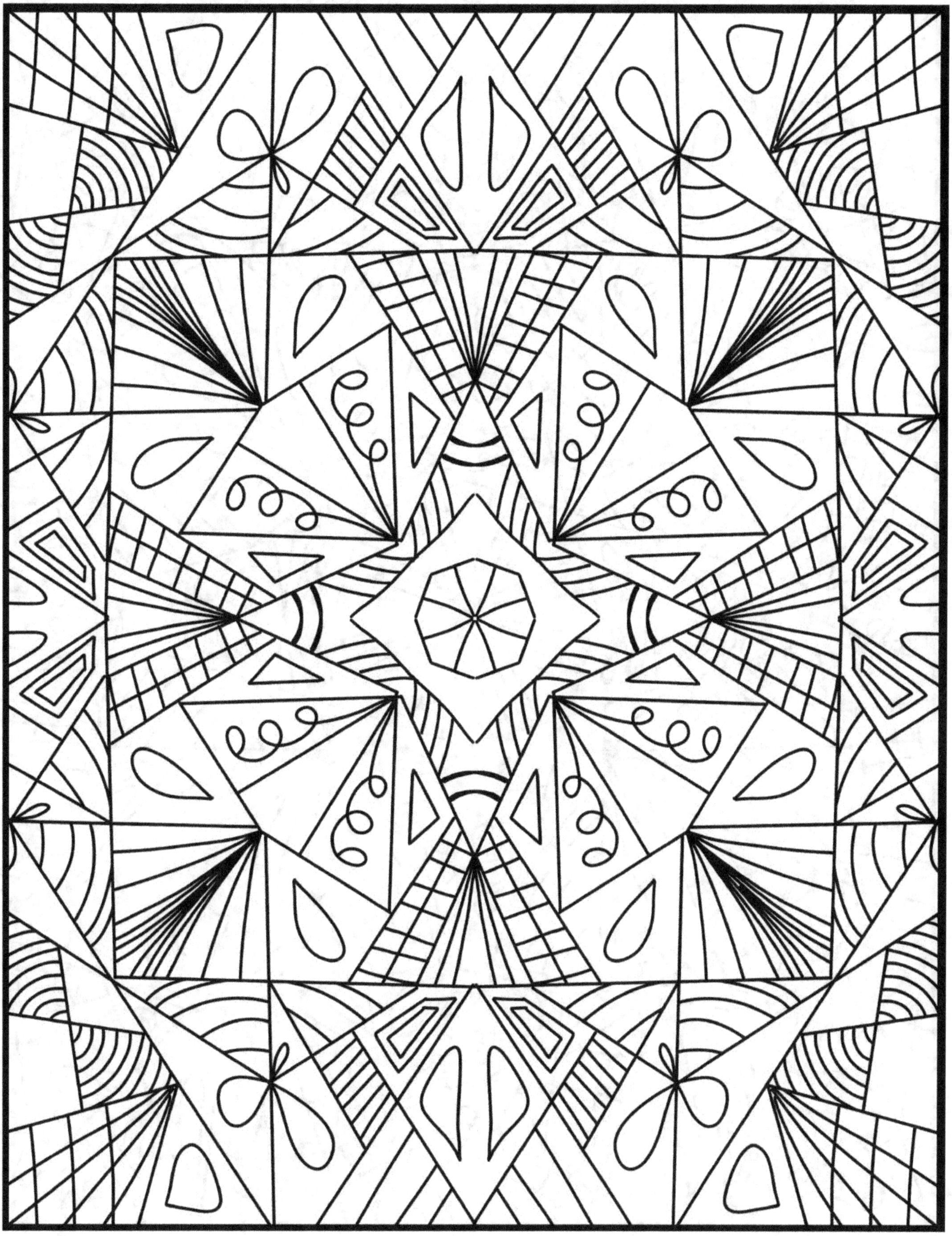

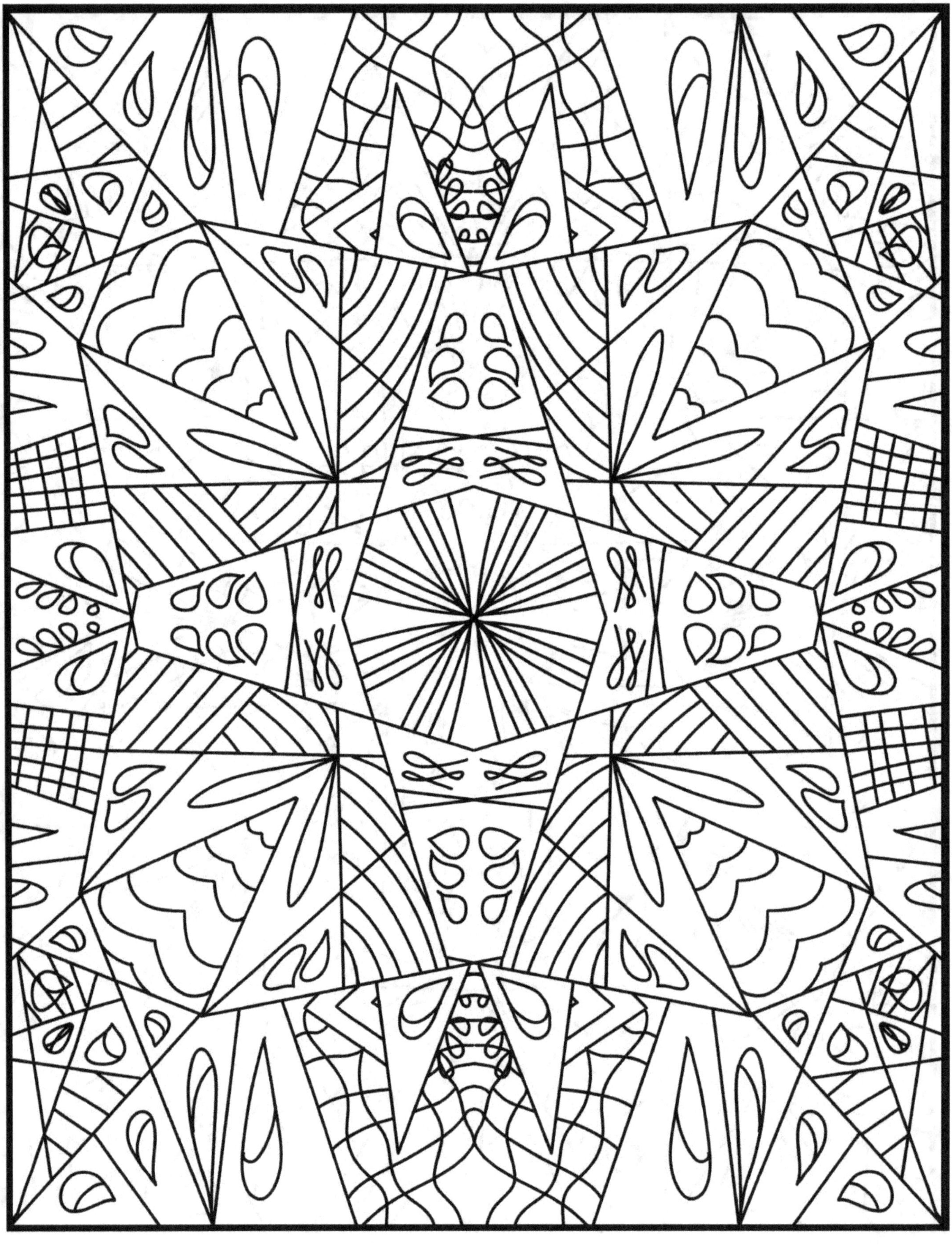

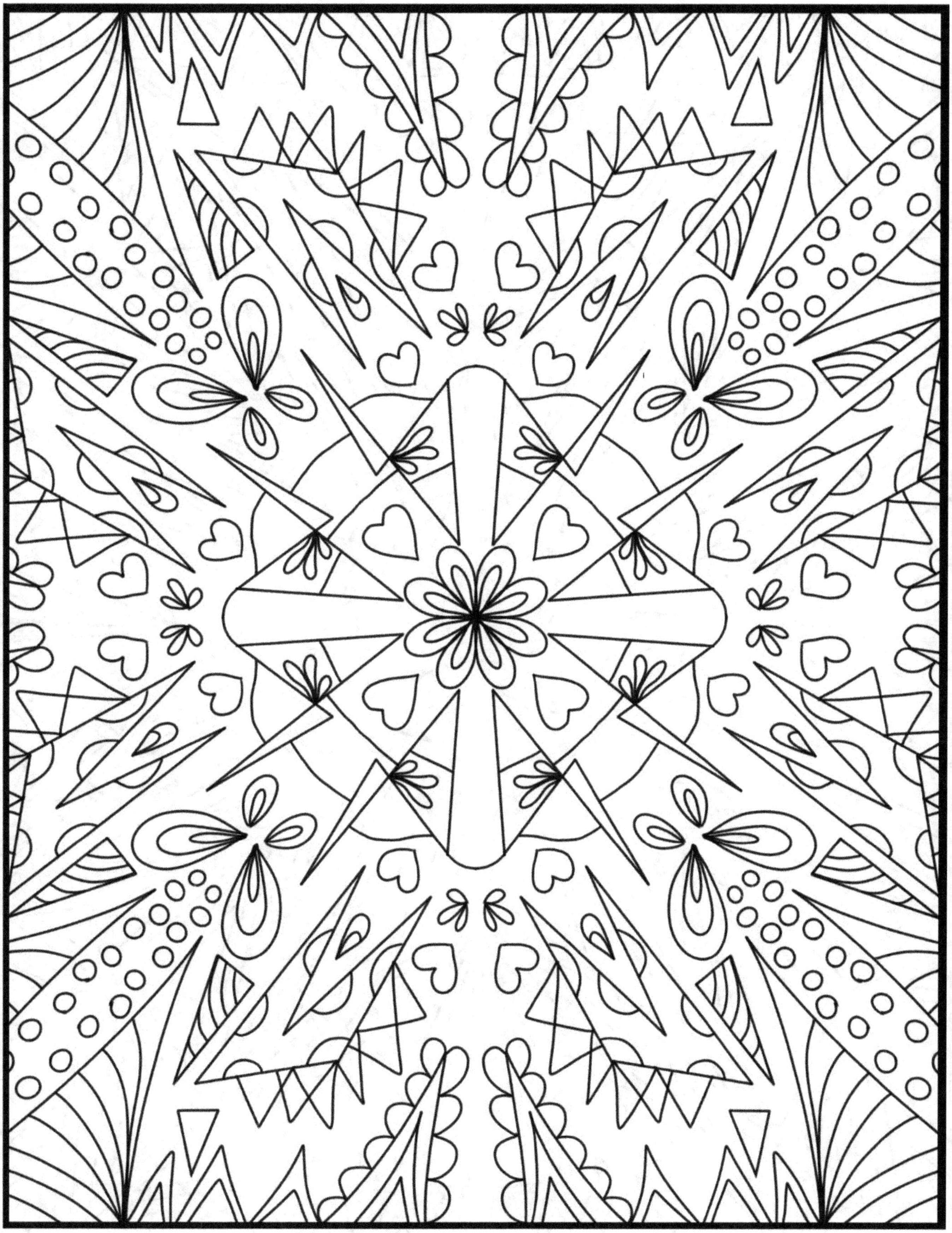

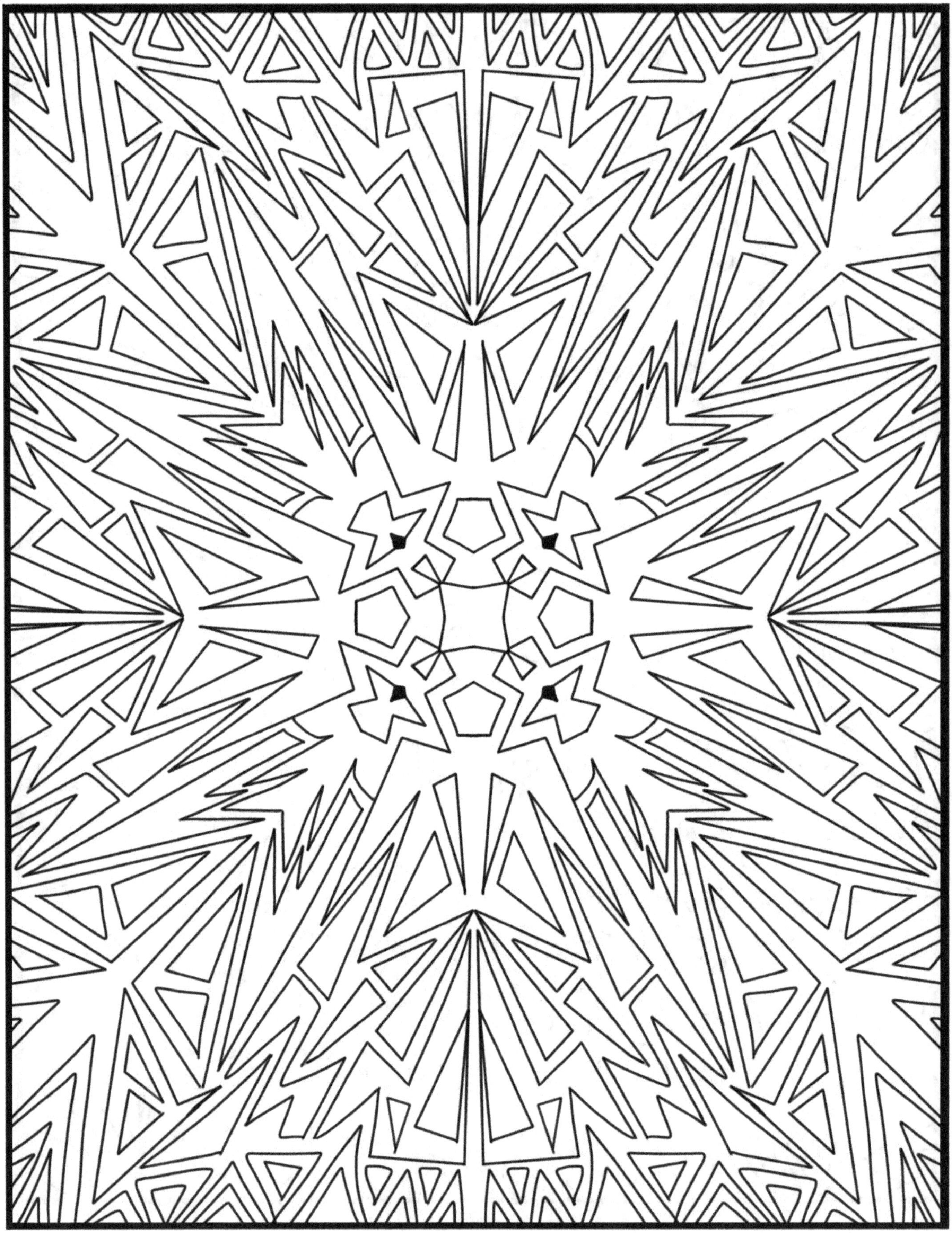

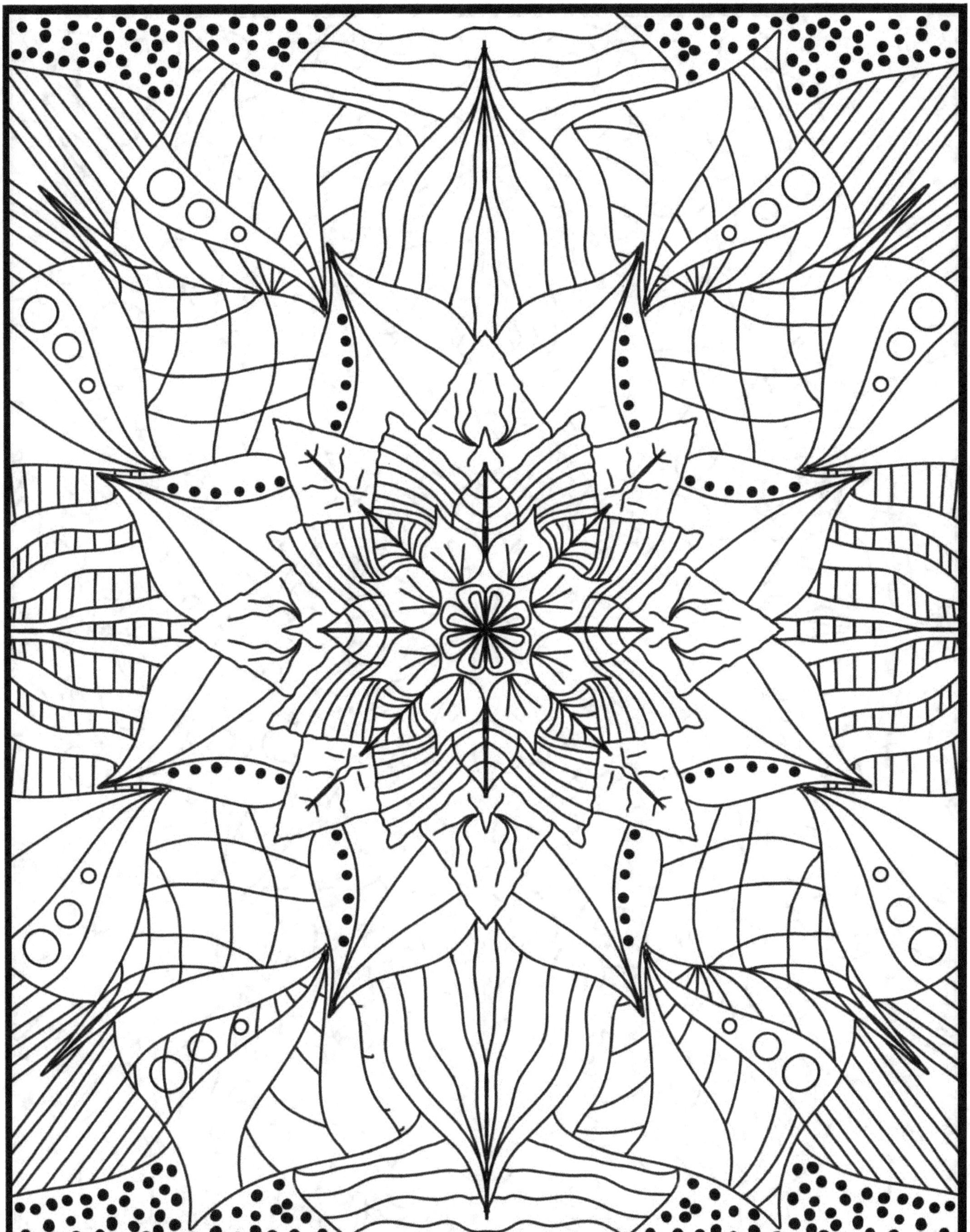

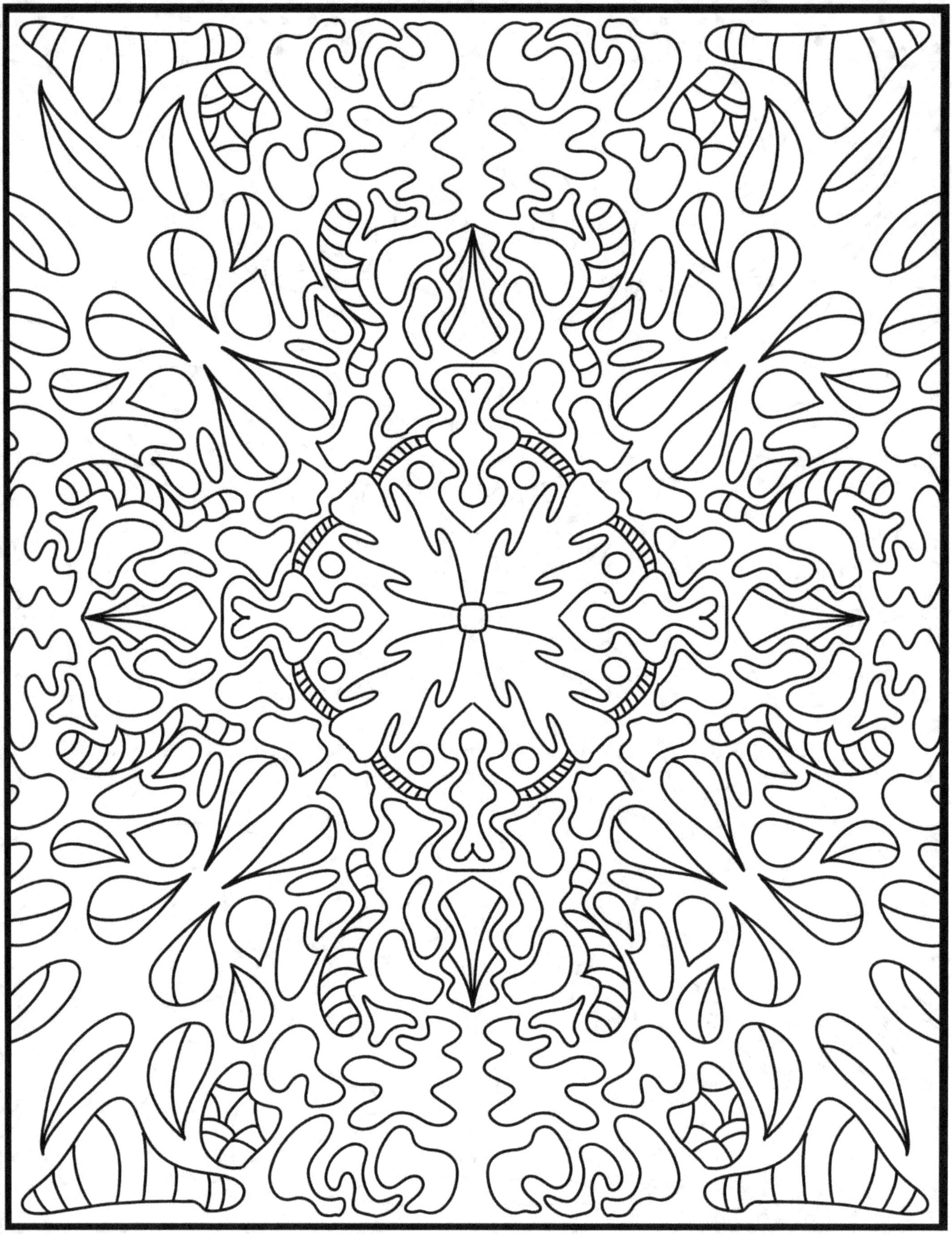

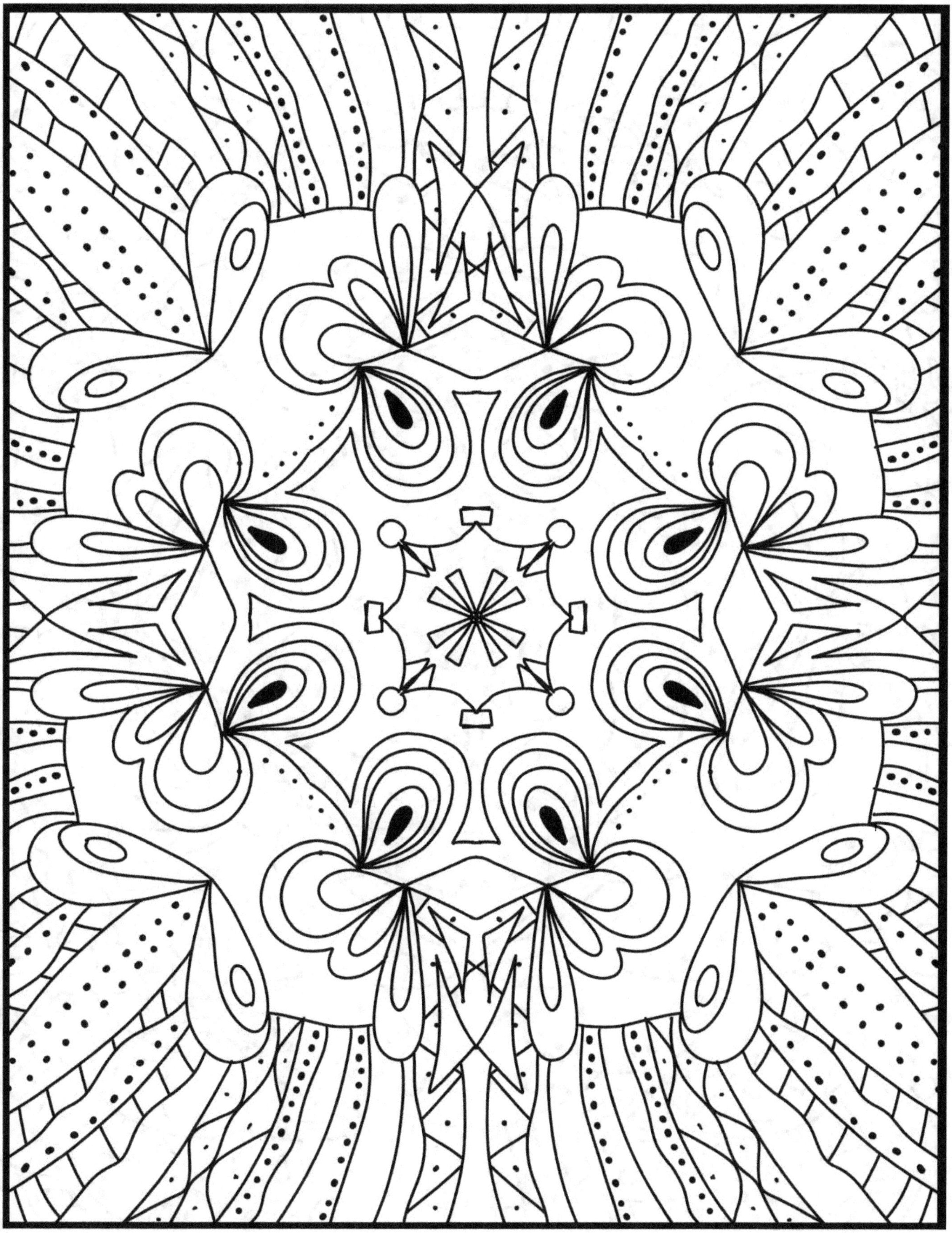

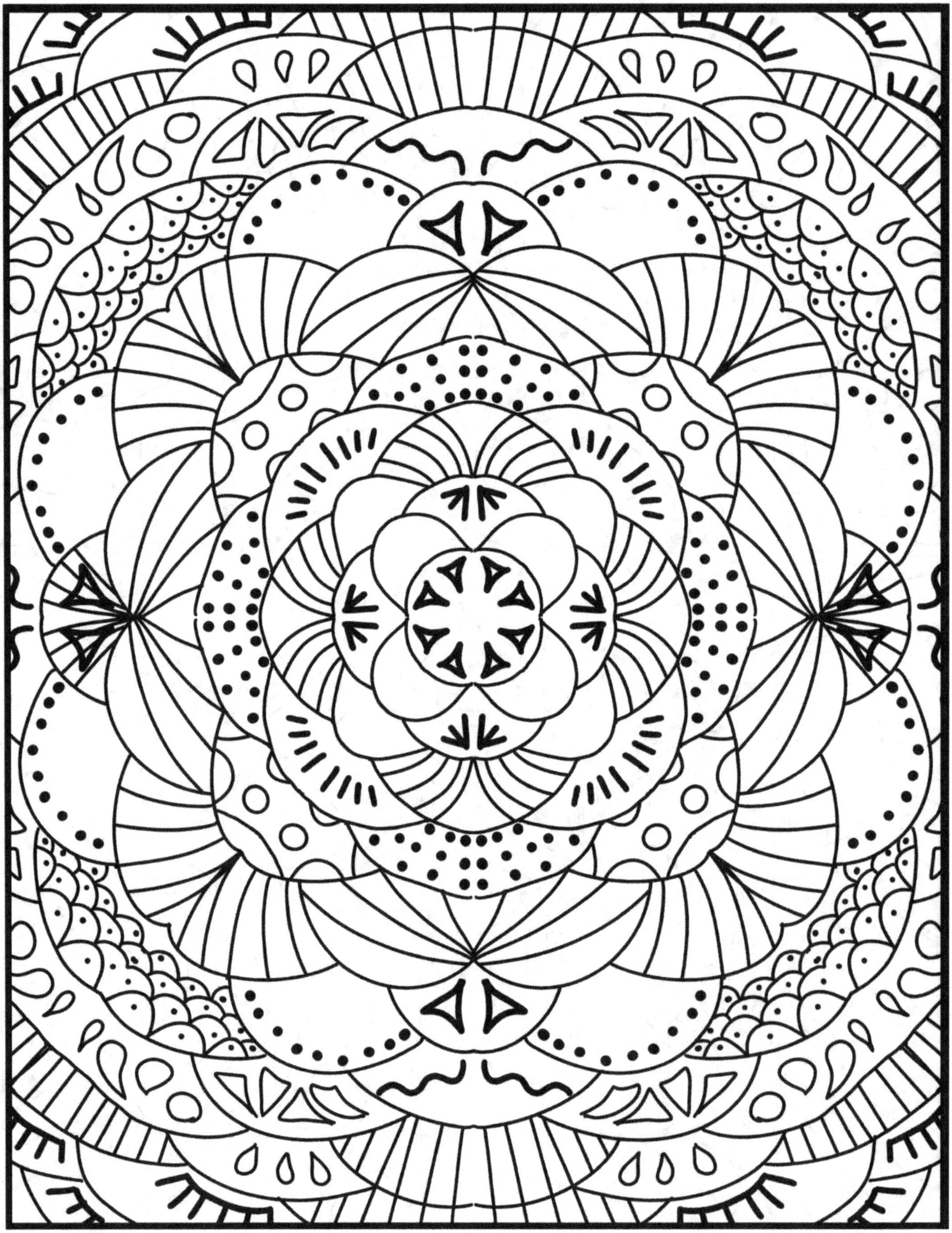

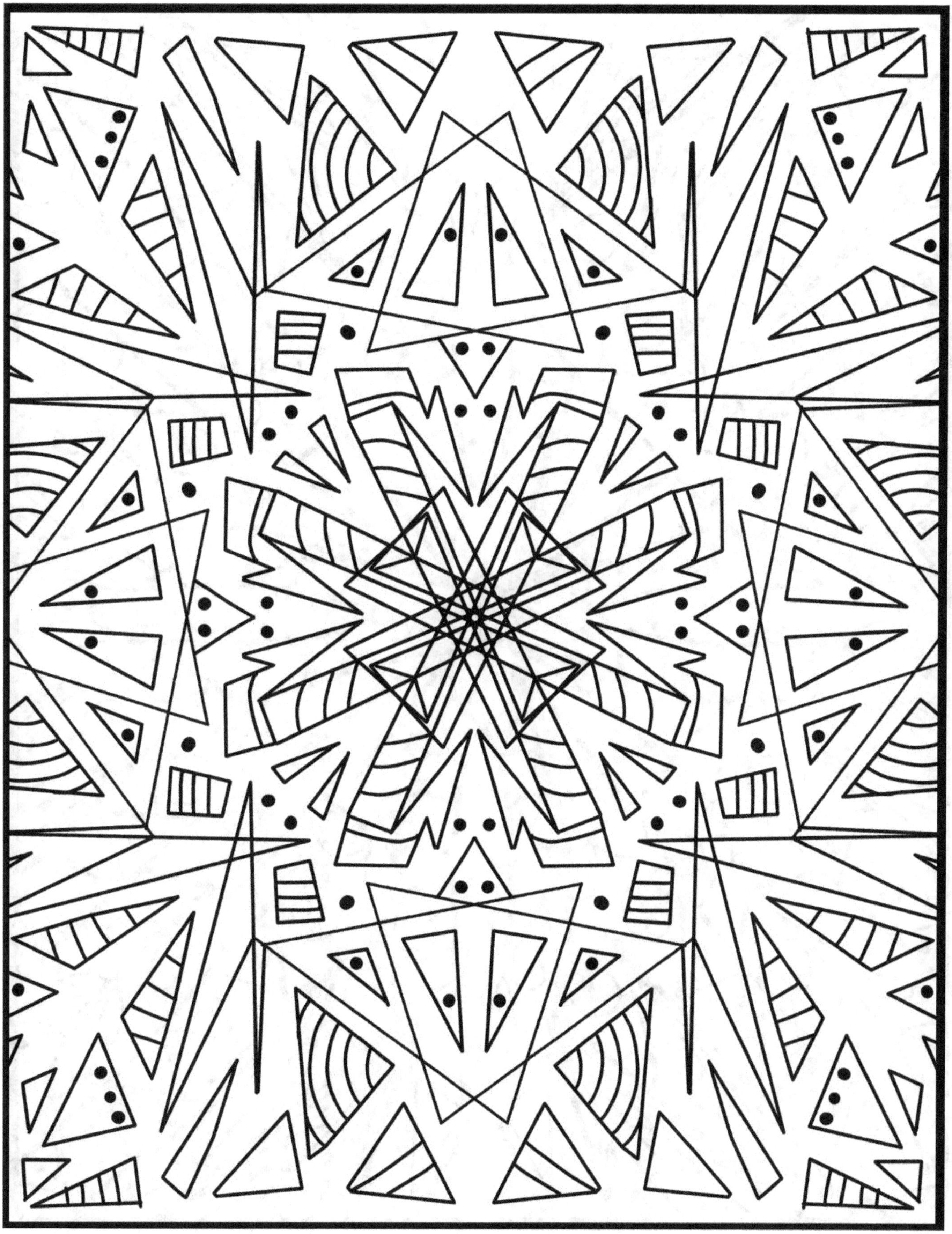

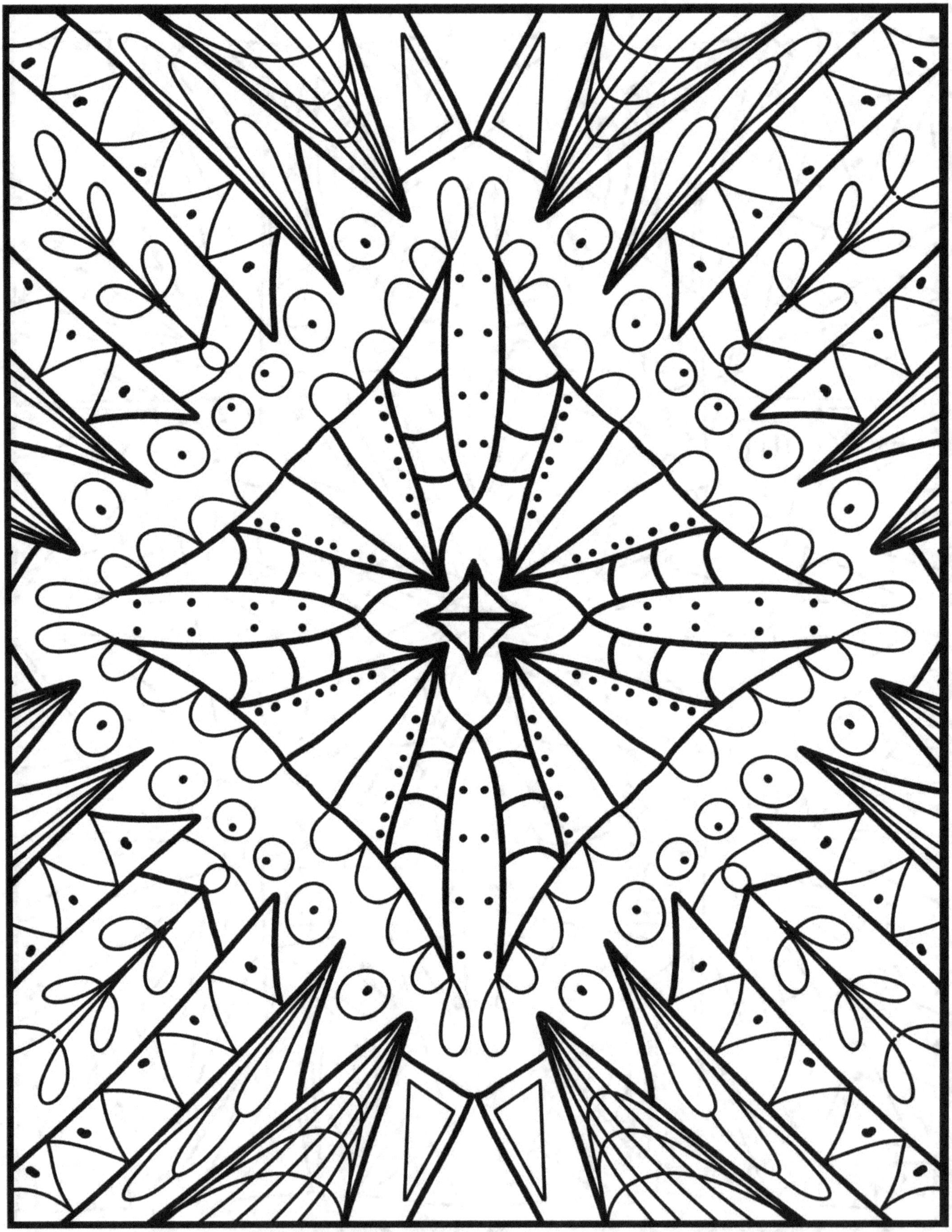

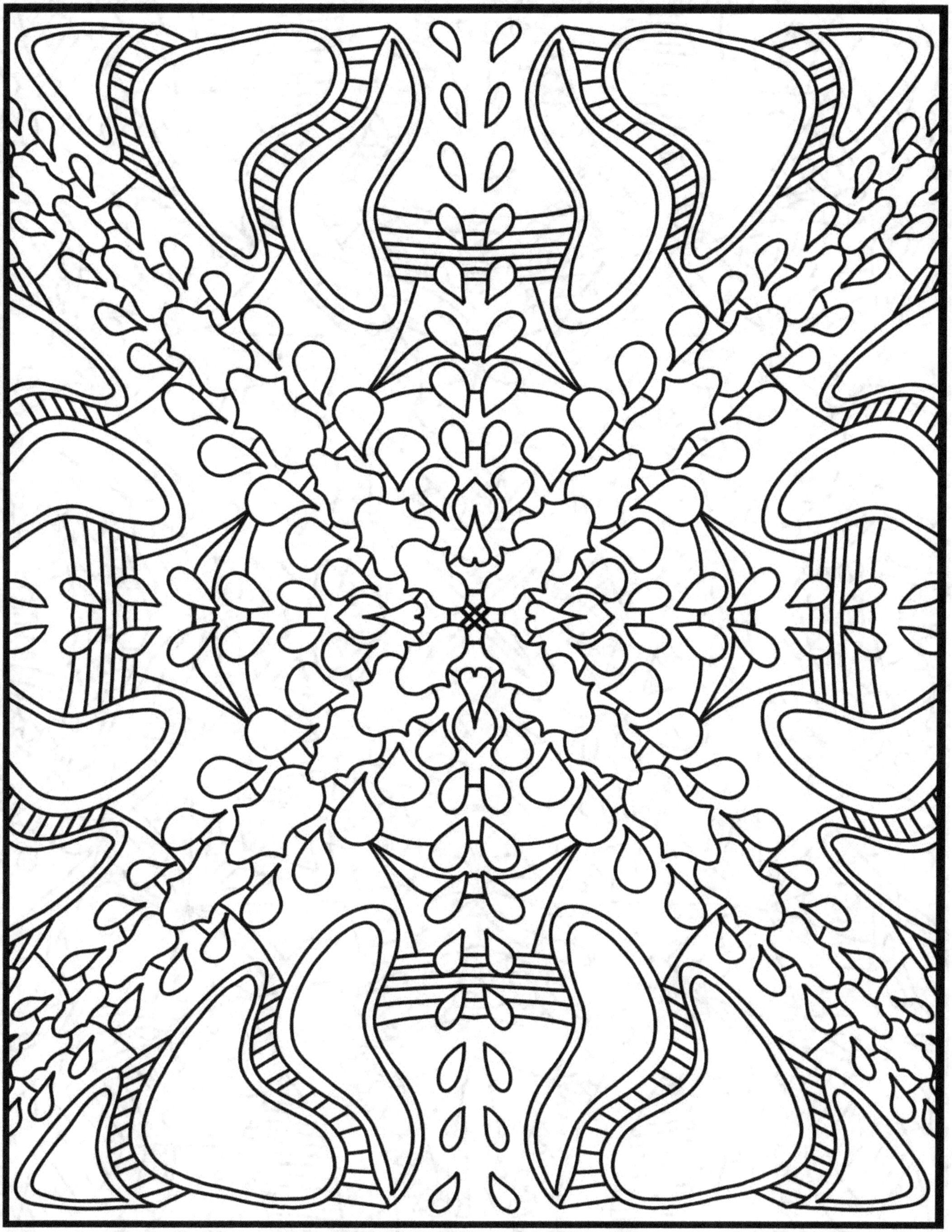

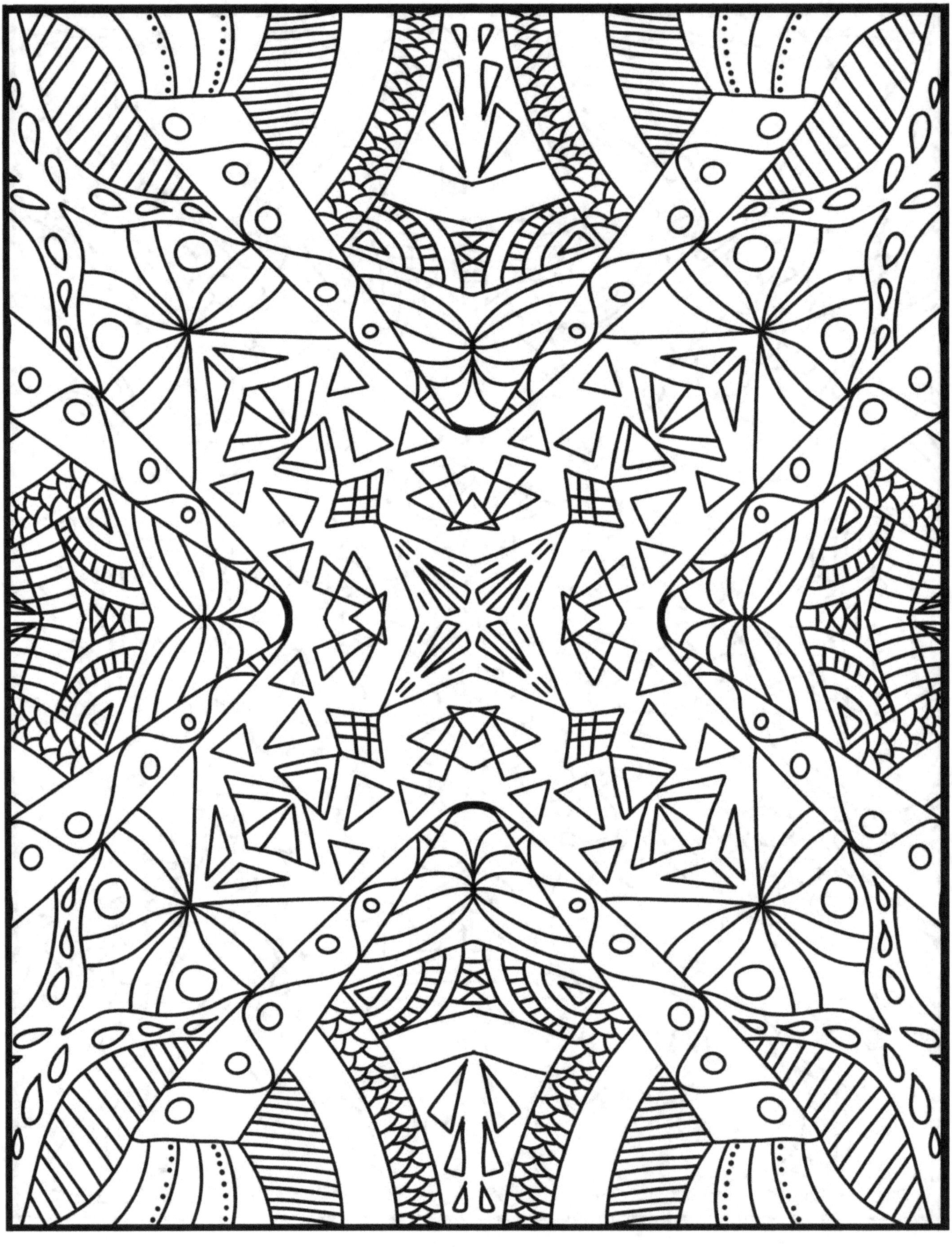

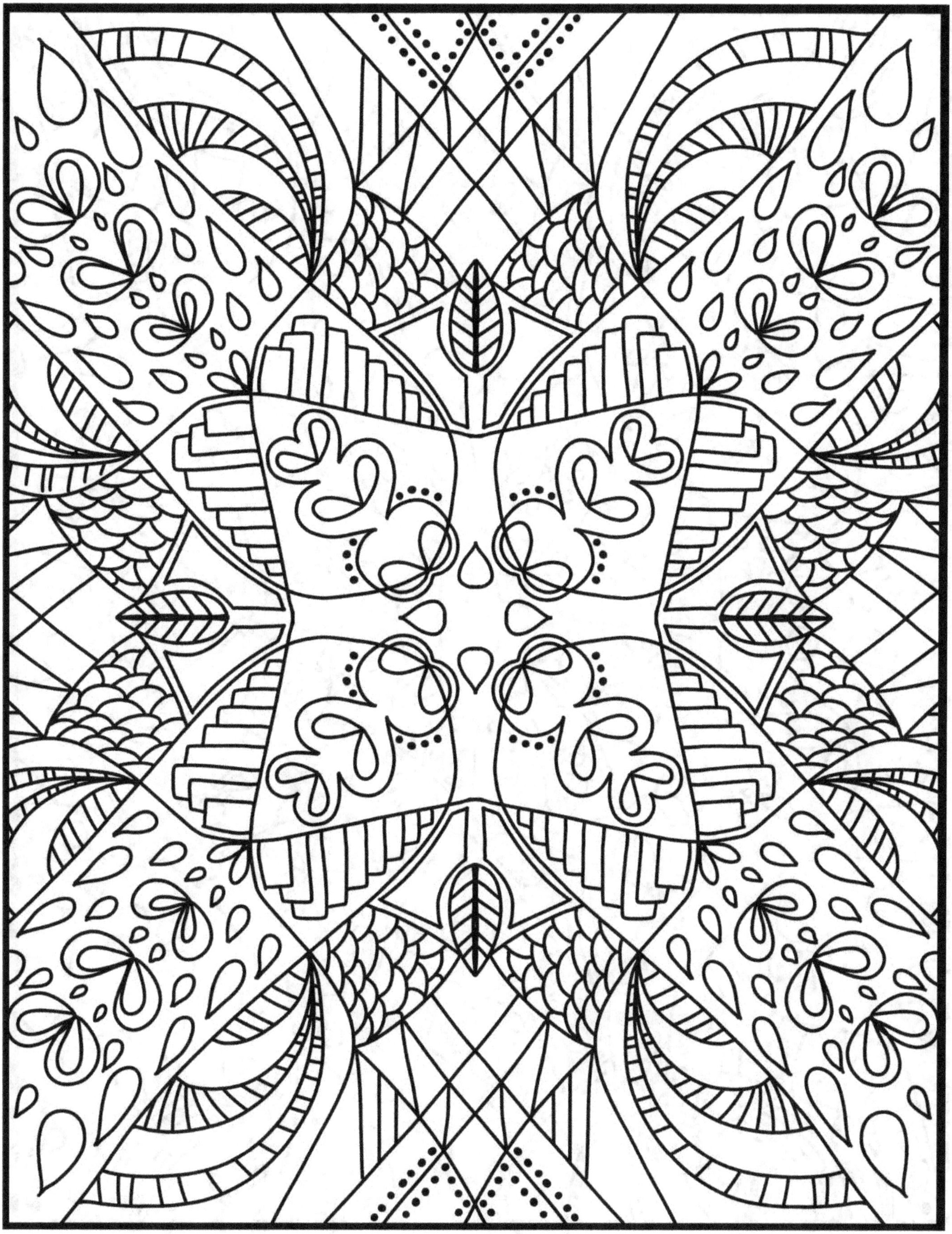

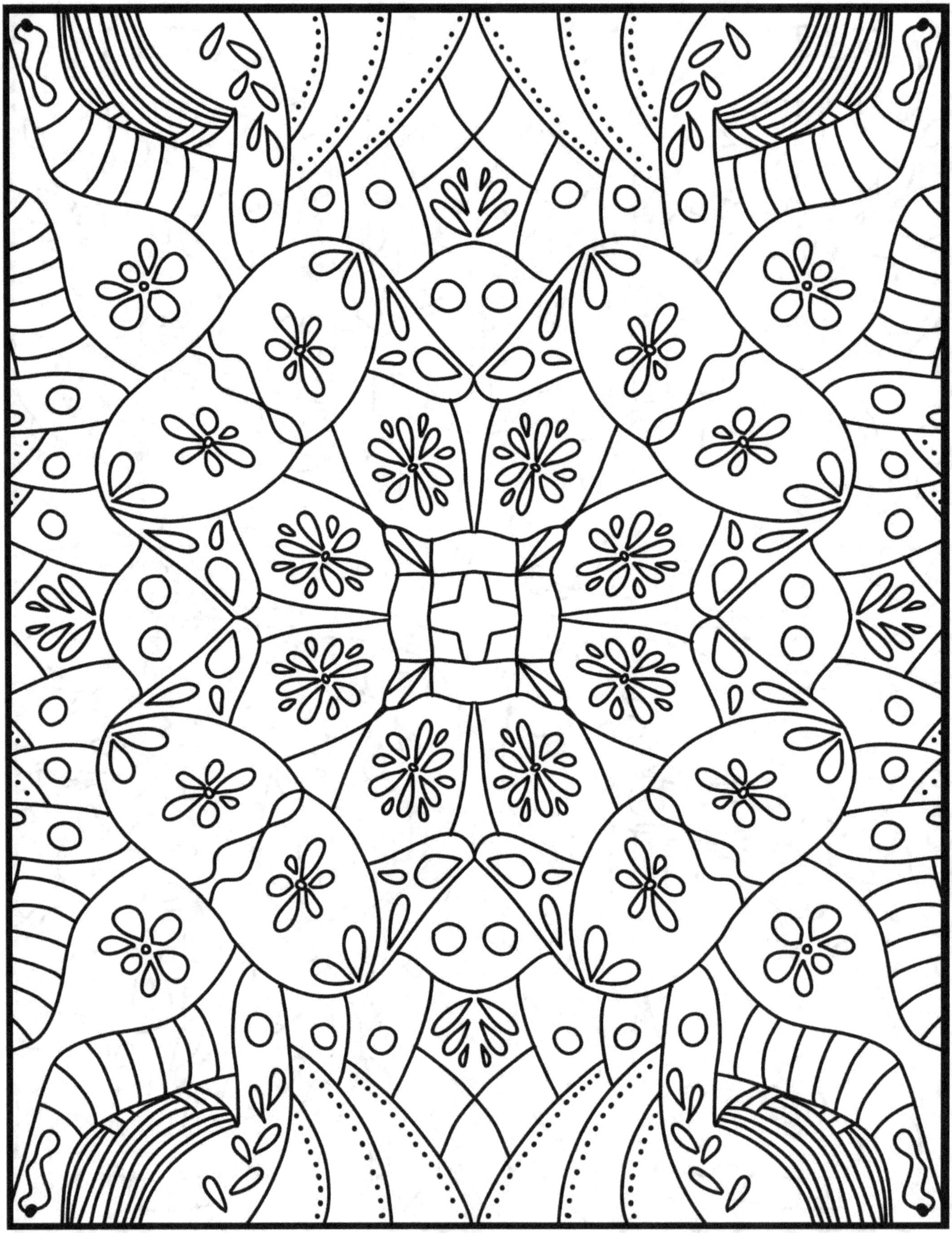

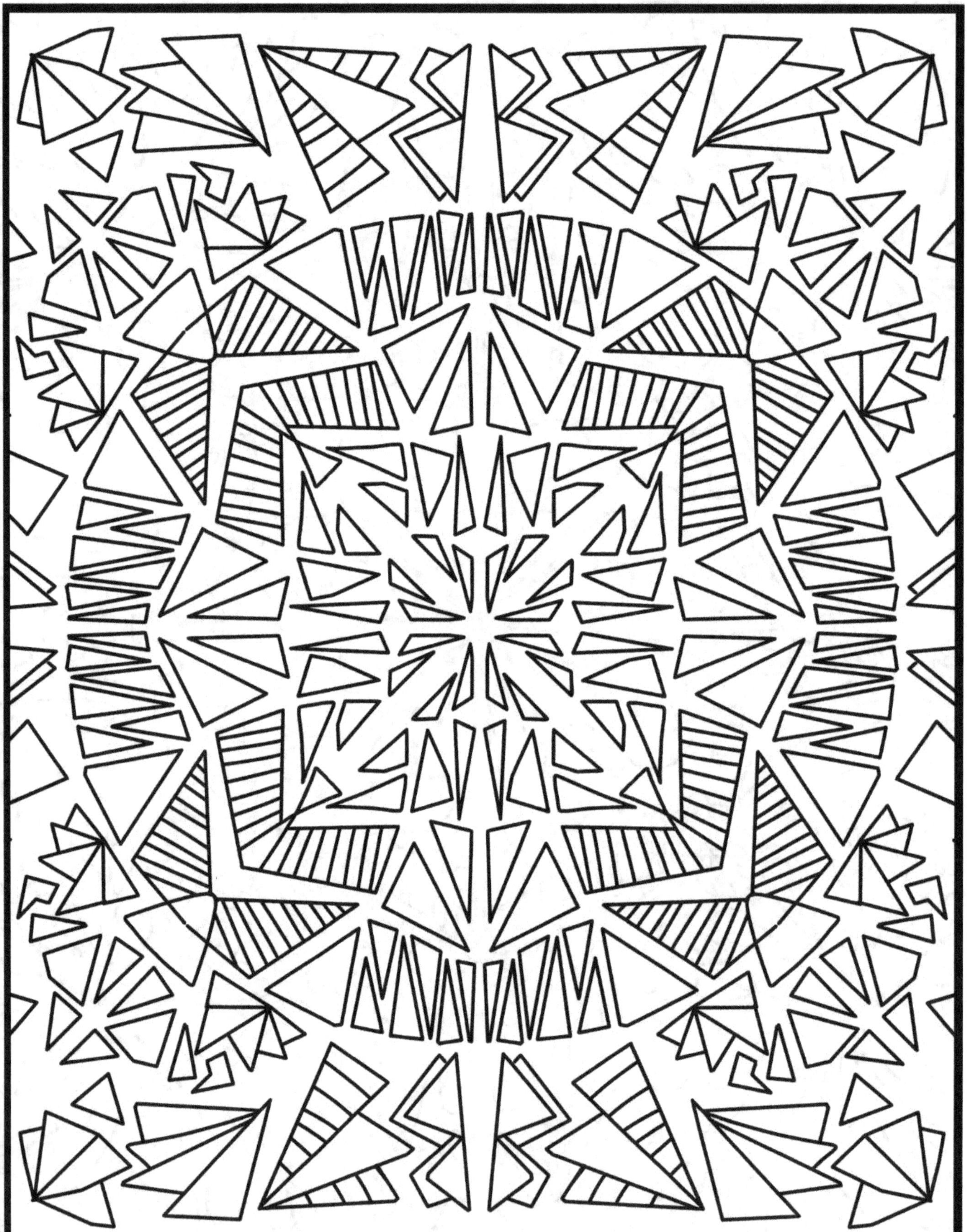

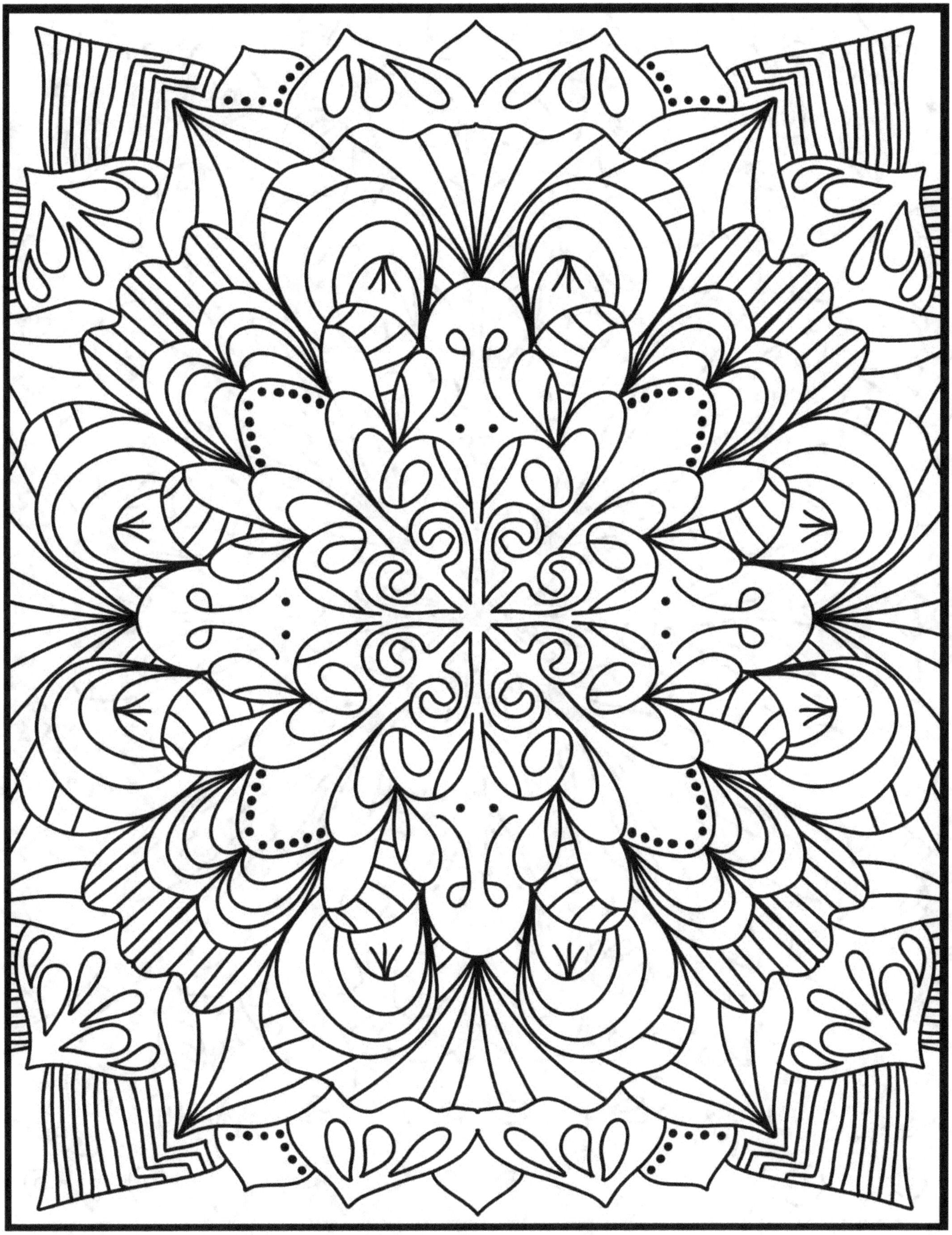

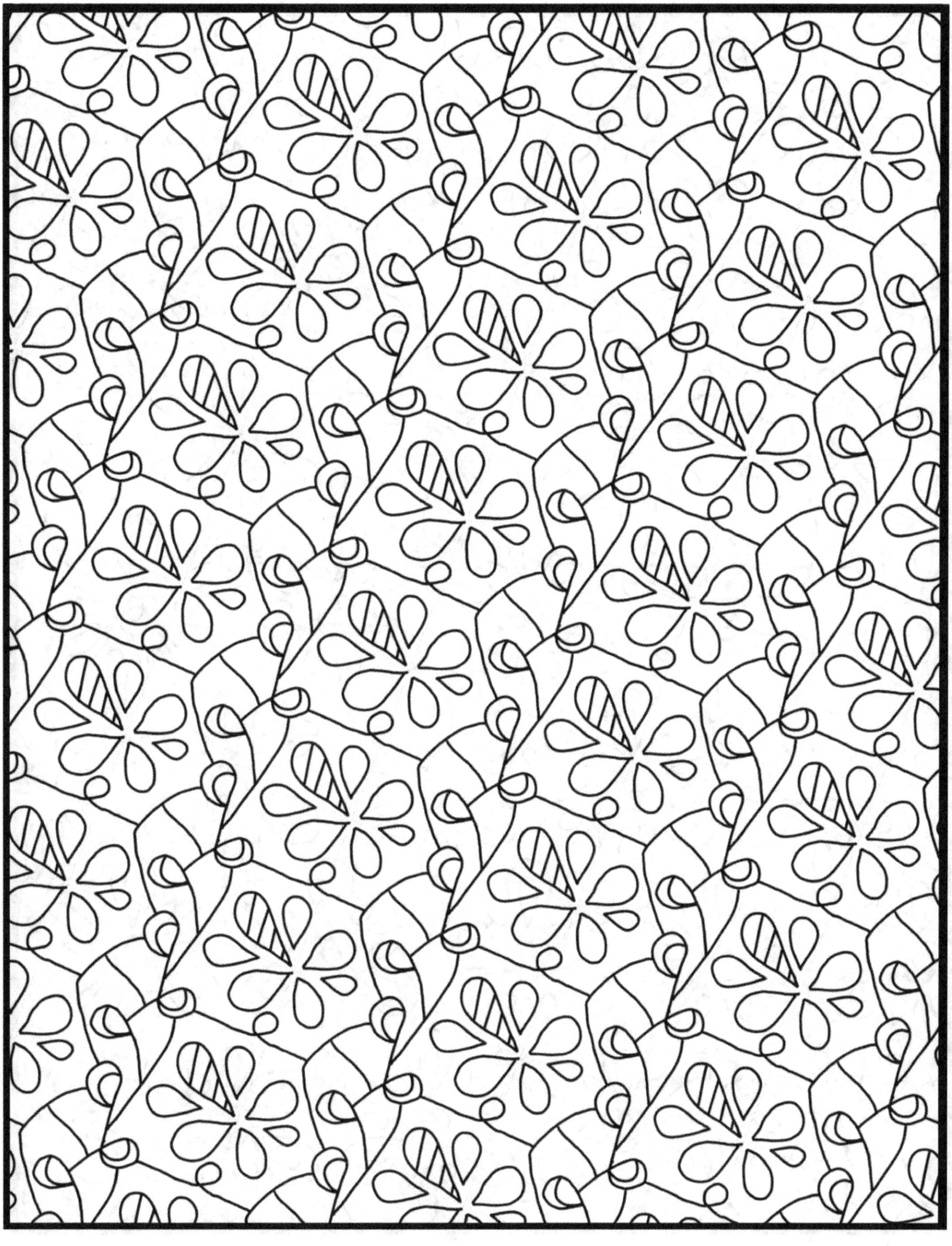

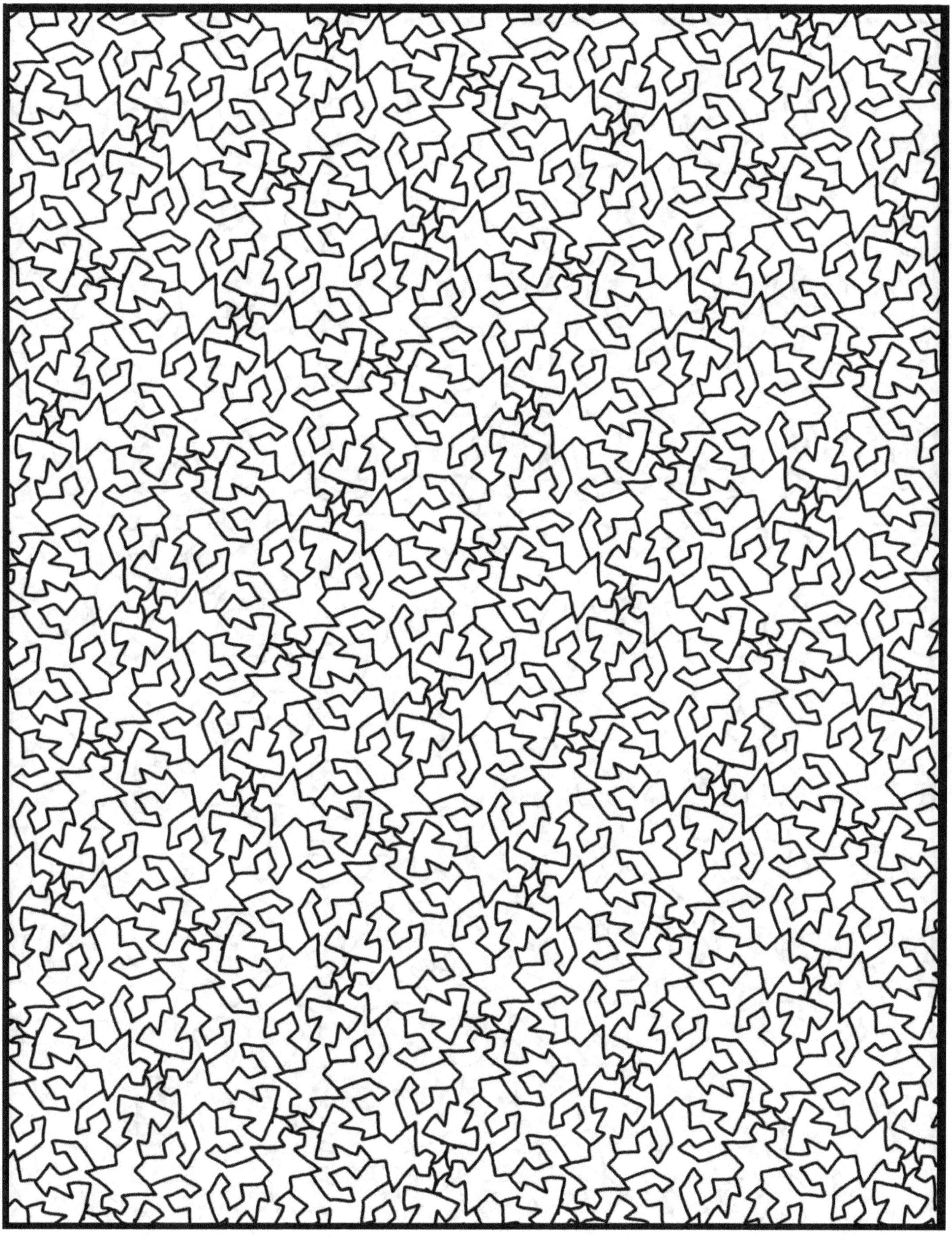

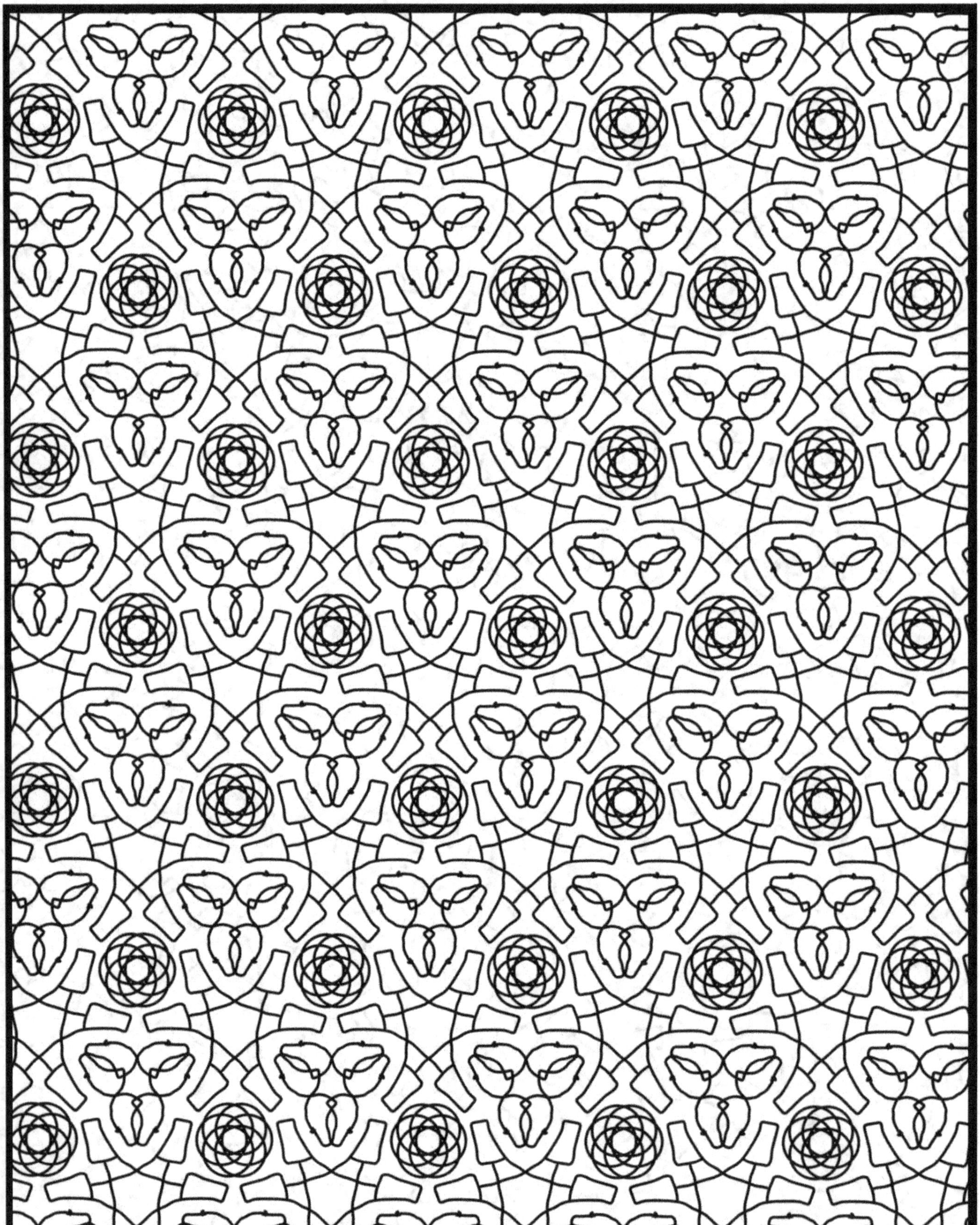

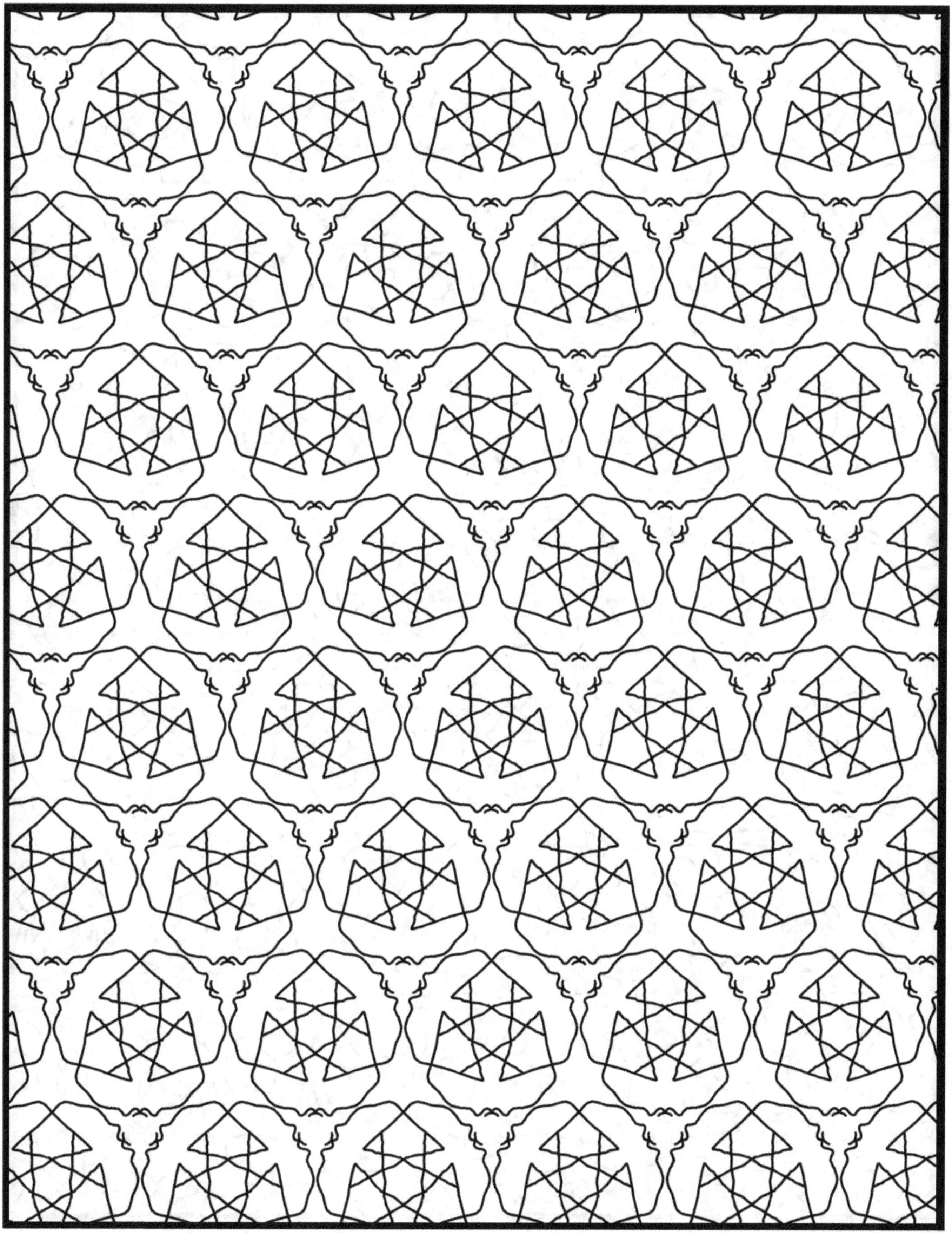

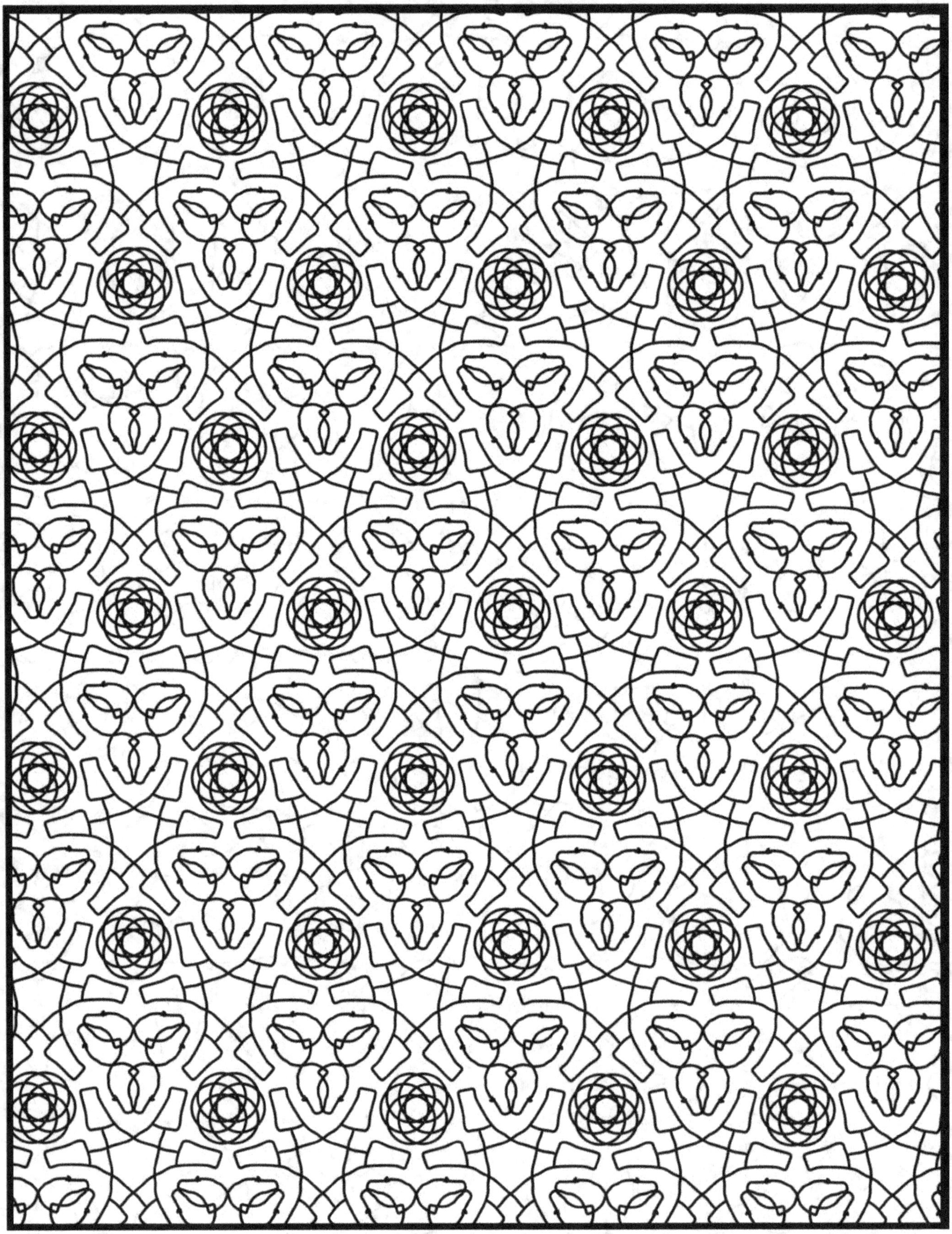

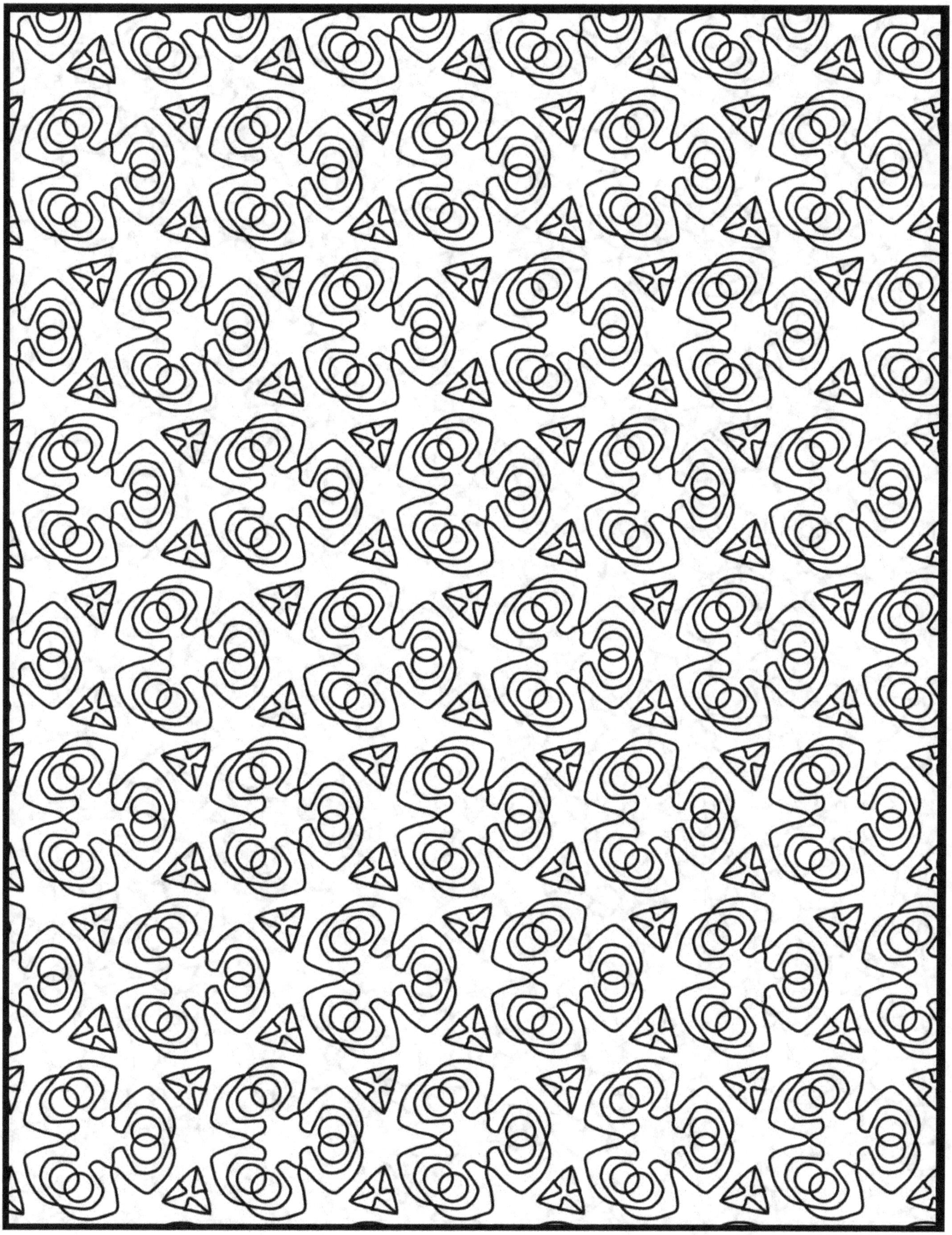

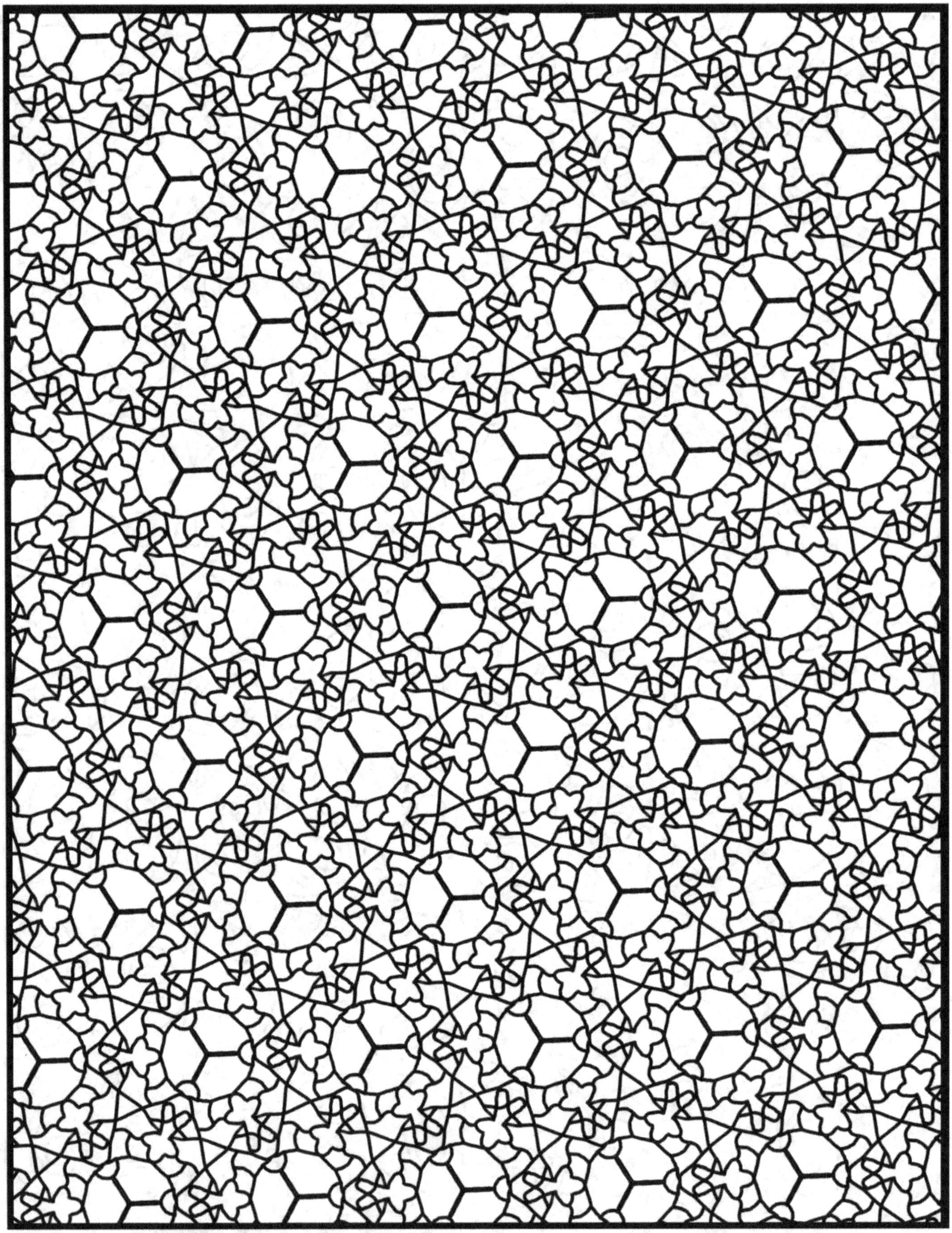

www.ingramcontent.com/pod-product-compliance
Lightning Source LLC
Chambersburg PA
CBHW081528220526
45467CB00010B/3088
* 9 7 9 8 7 1 0 1 6 6 2 0 8 *